W9-ABI-183

Online Addiction

The Internet

ReferencePoint
Press®

San Diego, CA

Other books in the Compact Research Internet set:

Cyberbullying
Cyberwarfare
The Digital Divide
Hacking

*For a complete list of titles please visit www.referencepointpress.com.

COMPACT *Research*

Online Addiction

Peggy J. Parks

The Internet

ReferencePoint
Press®

San Diego, CA

© 2013 ReferencePoint Press, Inc.
Printed in the United States

For more information, contact:
ReferencePoint Press, Inc.
PO Box 27779
San Diego, CA 92198
www.ReferencePointPress.com

Picture credits:
Maury Aaseng: 32–35, 47–49, 61–62, 75–76
AP Images: 17, 19

LIBRARY OF CONGRESS CATALOGING-IN-PUBLICATION DATA

Parks, Peggy J., 1951–
    Online addiction / by Peggy J. Parks.
        p. cm. -- (Compact research series)
    Includes bibliographical references and index.
    ISBN 978-1-60152-270-2 (hardback) -- ISBN 1-60152-270-3 (hardback)
1. Internet addiction--Popular works. I. Title.
    RC569.5.I54P37   2013
    616.85'84--dc23
                                                            2012014191

Contents

Foreword

“**Where is the knowledge we have lost in information?**”

—T.S. Eliot, “The Rock.”

As modern civilization continues to evolve, its ability to create, store, distribute, and access information expands exponentially. The explosion of information from all media continues to increase at a phenomenal rate. By 2020 some experts predict the worldwide information base will double every 73 days. While access to diverse sources of information and perspectives is paramount to any democratic society, information alone cannot help people gain knowledge and understanding. Information must be organized and presented clearly and succinctly in order to be understood. The challenge in the digital age becomes not the creation of information, but how best to sort, organize, enhance, and present information.

ReferencePoint Press developed the *Compact Research* series with this challenge of the information age in mind. More than any other subject area today, researching current issues can yield vast, diverse, and unqualified information that can be intimidating and overwhelming for even the most advanced and motivated researcher. The *Compact Research* series offers a compact, relevant, intelligent, and conveniently organized collection of information covering a variety of current topics ranging from illegal immigration and deforestation to diseases such as anorexia and meningitis.

The series focuses on three types of information: objective single-author narratives, opinion-based primary source quotations, and facts and statistics. The clearly written objective narratives provide context and reliable background information. Primary source quotes are carefully selected and cited, exposing the reader to differing points of view, and facts and statistics sections aid the reader in evaluating perspectives. Presenting these key types of information creates a richer, more balanced learning experience.

For better understanding and convenience, the series enhances information by organizing it into narrower topics and adding design features that make it easy for a reader to identify desired content. For example, in *Compact Research: Illegal Immigration*, a chapter covering the economic impact of illegal immigration has an objective narrative explaining the various ways the economy is impacted, a balanced section of numerous primary source quotes on the topic, followed by facts and full-color illustrations to encourage evaluation of contrasting perspectives.

The ancient Roman philosopher Lucius Annaeus Seneca wrote, "It is quality rather than quantity that matters." More than just a collection of content, the *Compact Research* series is simply committed to creating, finding, organizing, and presenting the most relevant and appropriate amount of information on a current topic in a user-friendly style that invites, intrigues, and fosters understanding.

Online Addiction at a Glance

Online Addiction Defined

Specialists define online addiction as compulsive Internet use to the point of interfering with someone's life and relationships.

A Controversial Disorder

Those who doubt that online addiction is real argue that one cannot become addicted to a behavior in the same way as to drugs and alcohol.

Prevalence

Reports on the incidence of online addiction vary widely, from less than 1 percent to nearly 38 percent, with the highest prevalence in Asian countries.

Risk Factors

People with low self-esteem, poor interpersonal skills, and below-average emotional maturity are said to be at high risk for becoming addicted to online activities.

Warning Signs

Excessive time spent on the computer is the most obvious sign of online addiction, combined with anxiety and irritability when the person is unable to be online.

Social Networking

Surveys have shown that many people who use online social networking feel as though they are unable to function if they cannot check Facebook and/or Twitter every day; experts say this could be a sign of addiction.

Online Gaming

Online addiction specialists say that online gaming, especially multiuser role-playing games, are some of the Internet's most addictive features.

Online Gambling

Cases of online gambling addiction appear to be on the rise, especially among teenagers and young adults.

Treatment Challenges

Online addiction is challenging to treat, largely because people either are in denial that they have a problem or do not want to give up their Internet activities.

Recovery

People who are addicted to Internet activities can recover, although specialized treatment facilities are scarce in the United States.

Overview

❝The internet has been a wonderful thing, enabling information sharing and a host of other activities to effortlessly take place. However, like all good things, the internet has a downside—one that can ruin lives and destroy families. It's called Internet Addiction.❞

—Lisa Haisha, a therapist from Los Angeles and founder of the humanitarian agency Whispers from Children's Hearts Foundation.

❝As we live in a world of growing dependence on technology, it is hard to tell the difference between necessity and addiction.❞

—Kimberly S. Young and Cristiano Nabuco de Abreu, psychologists and editors of the book *Internet Addiction: A Handbook and Guide to Evaluation and Treatment.*

Winston Ross, a journalist from Eugene, Oregon, is very familiar with online addiction. His knowledge stems not from the research he has done nor widespread publicity on the issue, but because of how the disorder has consumed his brother Andrew's life. Even though Andrew has never been formally diagnosed, Winston says that his brother "readily admits that he demonstrates all of the signs and symptoms of the compulsion." From the time Andrew was a teen, it was obvious that he felt most comfortable in the online world, as Winston writes: "His was a world of constant refreshing, immediate access to new information and stimuli. Before long, the real world couldn't hold his attention span. He dropped out of high school and spiraled down a path that eventually led him to homelessness."[1]

Although it disturbs Winston that his brother is homeless, Andrew seems relatively content with his chosen lifestyle. In a clearing ringed with blackberry bushes, between a set of railroad tracks and an Oregon highway, he sleeps atop three mattresses in a roomy tent. He goes to sleep and wakes up whenever he feels like it and spends nearly every waking moment in the nearby college computer lab. Once Andrew arrives at the lab in the morning, says Winston, "he'll spend the next 10 hours or so there, eyes focused on a computer screen. . . . He plays role-playing videogames such as World of Warcraft, but he's also got a page of RSS [web-tracking] feeds that makes my head spin, filled with blogs he's interested in, news Web sites, and other tentacles into cyberspace. He goes 'home' only when the lab closes." Winston worries about his brother and cannot help wondering if some kind of therapy could help him overcome his addiction and reconnect with the real world. "Then again," says Winston, "he's been consumed by computers for most of the past two decades. Maybe he's a lost cause."[2]

Hooked on Cyberspace

Since the early 1990s, when the launch of the World Wide Web made the Internet accessible to most anyone with a computer, the online population has soared. According to a report issued in January 2012 by the traffic and web analytics group Pingdom, over 2 billion people throughout the world actively use the Internet. This offers tremendous advantages and opportunities to users, from the ability to communicate at lightning speed to socializing, shopping, playing games, and hearing the latest news mere seconds after it happens. For some people, however, Internet use becomes compulsive, and they develop an unhealthy reliance on it—even to the point of its being the primary focus of their lives. According to mental health professionals, that is classic addictive behavior.

Online addiction (also called Internet addiction) is one of the

> " For some people . . . Internet use becomes compulsive, and they develop an unhealthy reliance on it—even to the point of its being the primary focus of their lives. "

behavioral addictions, meaning those that involve compulsive activities rather than physical dependence on alcohol and drugs. No formal criteria exist for online addiction, but mental health professionals who specialize in the disorder define it as uncontrollable, compulsive, heavy use of the Internet that results in a significant negative impact on someone's life. British psychologist Mark D. Griffiths, who is a noted expert on behavioral addictions, writes: "In a nutshell, the fundamental difference between excessive enthusiasm and addiction is that healthy enthusiasms add to life whereas addiction takes away from it."[3]

Is Online Addiction Real?

As reports of online addiction have spiked in recent years, the disorder has become an issue of controversy among mental health professionals. At the heart of the dispute is whether even the most excessive use of the Internet can be considered a true addiction, as Australian psychiatrist Philip Tam explains: "There is heated debate within my profession as to whether this is a real mental condition, deserving of diagnosis, research and treatment, or simply a form of human behaviour responding to the huge changes brought about by the 'internet revolution' of the past 2 decades."[4]

> **Despite increasing reports of online addiction, health officials have no way of knowing how many people suffer from it.**

The American Psychiatric Association (APA) does not formally acknowledge Internet addiction as a mental disorder, nor is it included in the group's *Diagnostic and Statistical Manual of Mental Disorders* (DSM). The DSM contains specific criteria for all mental disorders and serves as a guideline for clinicians to use when diagnosing patients. The most recent DSM was published in 2000 and a new edition (the DSM-V) was slated for release in 2013. Plans for the DSM-V called for replacing substance abuse and dependence with addiction and related disorders, which includes behavioral (nonsubstance) addictions. The APA opted not to include Internet addiction in this section, however, as a 2010 news release stated: "While 'internet addiction' was considered for inclusion in this category, the work group decided there was insufficient research data to do so. They are recommending it be included in the manual's appendix instead, with a goal of encouraging additional study."[5]

All Walks of Life

Online addiction does not discriminate. It affects people of all ages, ethnicities, and income levels, in countries throughout the world. Cases range from teenagers obsessed with social networking or online gaming to adults who sacrifice time with their families in order to spend hour after hour in front of a computer screen. Psychiatrists Timothy Liu and Marc N. Potenza write: "Problematic Internet use occurs in a wide variety of individuals—new and savvy users, adolescent and middle-aged individuals, men and women, those with comorbid [accompanying] psychiatric disorders and those without, those who cannot function or work and those who appear to have relatively high functioning."[6]

> Another significant risk factor for online addiction is a preexisting mental illness, as up to 85 percent of Internet addicts have been shown to suffer from one or more other mental disorders.

Despite increasing reports of online addiction, health officials have no way of knowing how many people suffer from it. In his 2011 book *Virtually You*, psychiatrist and Internet addiction expert Elias Aboujaoude explains: "Depending on the definition used, the population studied, and the quality of the research, Internet addiction rates have varied widely—from 0.3 percent in a U.S. population survey to nearly 38 percent in a study of Hong Kong teenagers and young adults."[7] One of the most comprehensive studies of online addiction was conducted in 2006 by Aboujaoude and his colleagues from Stanford University and involved telephone interviews with over 2,500 adults throughout the United States. The study revealed that from 4 to 14 percent were problematic Internet users, with 6 percent admitting that their personal relationships had suffered as a consequence.

A more recent study was conducted by a team of researchers led by

Dimitri A. Christakis, a professor of pediatrics at the University of Washington School of Public Health. The team analyzed Internet use among students at two major American universities and determined that 4 percent either had problematic Internet use or were addicted to their online activities. In a 2011 report of the study, the authors write: "To put the prevalence in perspective . . . problematic Internet usage would be as common as asthma in a similar population of children."[8]

Risk Factors

Mental health experts have identified factors that can increase someone's risk of developing online addiction, including low self-esteem, poor interpersonal skills, and below-average emotional maturity. People who have one or more of these qualities often find it more comfortable to socialize online rather than in person. In trying to compensate for their lack of real-life relationships, they risk becoming overly dependent on the Internet. According to psychologist and online addiction expert Kimberly S. Young, this is an important element of some people's obsession with eBay. When an individual is repeatedly a winning bidder or successful seller on the auction site, this could fulfill unmet emotional needs, as Young explains: "In many cases, addicted users suffer from low self-esteem and winning makes them feel important and they gain personal recognition if they become a highly rated 'power seller.'"[9]

> In keeping with their secretive behavior, it is not unusual for online addicts to lie about how much time they spend on the computer.

Another significant risk factor for online addiction is a preexisting mental illness, as up to 85 percent of Internet addicts have been shown to suffer from one or more other mental disorders. Examining this connection was one focus of a study published in October 2009 by a group of researchers from Taiwan. The team concluded that young people with attention-deficit/hyperactivity disorder, social phobia, depression, or hostility have a higher-than-normal risk of becoming addicted to the Internet. Also at high risk are those who are struggling to overcome other types of addiction, as Young explains: "Many Internet Addicts openly admit to having an 'addictive personality' and previously abused prescription medication, alcohol, cigarettes, or food."[10]

Signs of Trouble

People who become overly dependent on Internet activities often go out of their way to hide the problem from others. In his book *Cyber Junkies*, Kevin Roberts explains that Internet addicts "steal away to secret locations to pursue pleasure peacefully—away from prying eyes and inquisitive minds. Like most addicts, we hide our behavior."[11] Roberts speaks from experience because he had a long, difficult battle with online addiction. He says there is a reason why Internet "junkies" go out of their way to keep their obsession to themselves: "Openly displaying our tendency to game excessively or obsess over our social networking site profiles has resulted in scolding and criticism."[12]

In keeping with their secretive behavior, it is not unusual for online addicts to lie about how much time they spend on the computer. According to a January 2010 article by the addiction treatment facility Elements Behavioral Health, this is common among teenagers who suffer from compulsive Internet use. The group writes: "Asked about the amount of time spent online, what they were doing, or confronted with evidence on cell phone bills for texting, IMs, or downloading, your teen gives you elaborate and fabricated [explanations]—all in an attempt to divert your attention from the fact that he or she is spending way too much time online."[13] Other symptoms of online addiction among young people include emotional outbursts when confronted about excessive computer use, chronic fatigue from little sleep, and a drop in grades.

One of the most obvious signs that someone has become a compulsive Internet user is how he or she feels and acts when the Internet is not accessible. Online addiction experts say the anxiety and irritability that are common under these circumstances is much like withdrawal symptoms suffered by drug addicts who cannot get drugs. Referring to a patient who admitted his addiction to online activities, Aboujaoude writes: "He knew how difficult it can be to sever one's Internet connection. When he tried to do it, or when his server would fail without forewarning, he experienced significant 'withdrawal,' a state of heightened anxiety and physical restlessness familiar to heavy smokers who try to quit cold turkey."[14]

Can People Get Addicted to Social Networking?

With over 900 million members worldwide, and a user population composed of everyone from preteens to octogenarians, Facebook is the number-one-rated social networking site. Most people who use Facebook, as well as Tumblr, Twitter, and YouTube, are able to balance the amount of time they spend online with their real-world hobbies and activities. A certain percentage, however, have developed an unhealthy attachment to social networking, which specialists say is a warning sign of addiction. New York psychologist Michael Fenichel writes:

> Add to the instant texting component the ability to post pictures and videos, play pop-psychology games and pop-culture games and quizzes . . . follow (slightly less closely than Twitter) the every move, decision, feeling, and random thought of everyone in countless networks, and also maintain a homepage/wall for all to see and visit, and this is the best possible recipe for significant (behavioral) addiction, as it fills a large and "normal" part of so many lives.[15]

Erin Clark, an actress from New York City, is a classic example of someone who is obsessed with online activities, especially social networking. "I spend maybe 75 percent of my day online," she says, "checking e-mail, casting websites, MySpace, and Facebook. Then I'll circle back and recheck all of them continuously. On many nights, I've stayed up until 4 a.m. doing this." Clark finds it hard to communicate any way other than online, and her career and relationships have suffered because of it. "It's just easier for me to stay behind a computer screen than deal with small talk," she says. "A few months ago, I said I'd attend a friend's performance, but at the last minute I decided to stay home and surf the Web. I barely talk to some of my best friends, and if I do, it's through Facebook."[16]

How Serious a Problem Is Compulsive Online Gaming and Gambling?

Online games, particularly multiuser role-playing games such as *World of Warcraft*, *EverQuest*, and *Final Fantasy*, have been called some of the Internet's most addictive features. People of all ages get hooked on these games, but teens and young adults have been identified as having the

A college student delves into the World of Warcraft *game in his off hours. Teens and young adults are especially susceptible to the addictive qualities of online role-playing games such as* World of Warcraft.

highest risk for addiction. Scientist Karen M. von Deneen explains: "In online games you can become a hero, build empires, and submerge yourself in a fantasy. That kind of escapism is what draws young people."[17]

Kevin Roberts escaped into the fantasy world of gaming and became hopelessly addicted to it. When he was in college, Roberts discovered the online role-playing game *Sid Meier's Civilization* and was immediately hooked. He estimates that over a two-month period, he spent nearly 500 hours in the school's computer lab playing the game. He lied to people about what he was doing, saying that he was working on a project for one of his classes, as he explains: "I led friends to believe that I had been researching political theory at the graduate library." As is typical for compulsive online gamers, Roberts became so immersed in his game playing that it consumed his time and became more of a priority than anything

> **Online games, particularly multiuser role-playing games such as *World of Warcraft*, *EverQuest*, and *Final Fantasy*, have been called some of the Internet's most addictive features.**

else in his life. "Answering machine messages included invitations to hit the beach, attend parties, and take road trips," he says. "I called no one back and engaged in none of these previously satisfying activities."[18]

Internet gambling has not been around as long as online gaming, but its popularity is growing fast, especially among teens and young adults—and with this growth has come increased reports of gambling addiction. Young refers to "a new breed of gambling addicts," as she writes: "Young adults who seek admission to an online [gambling] site can freely enter, as no one is there to check for proof of age or an ID."[19] According to Young, compulsive online gambling has been identified as a growing problem on college campuses. Students have been discovered using their Internet privileges to gamble, which has caused concern among school officials.

Asian Epidemic

Unlike in the United States, health professionals in some Asian countries do not view online addiction as a controversy—they view it as a crisis. According to Liu and Potenza, Internet addiction is most prominent in South Korea, Taiwan, and China, where "problematic Internet use is considered one of the most serious public health issues by the governments of these countries."[20] In South Korea, which is often called the most wired nation in the world, government authorities conducted two major surveys between 2010 and 2011. They were stunned to find that at least one in 20 adolescents suffered from severe Internet addiction, with one in 10 at high risk for becoming addicted.

Because of the seriousness of online addiction in South Korea, government officials are desperately seeking answers. One effort, which is intended to stop the problem before it starts, was the April 2011 passage of nighttime shutdown legislation. Often referred to as the Cinderella law, it forces gaming companies to block users aged 16 and under from playing online games at any location between midnight and 6:00 a.m.

Officials in China are also seeking solutions to online addiction because the problem is growing rapidly there, too. In February 2010 the China Youth Internet Association announced that an estimated 24 million Chinese youths were addicted to online activities, most notably gaming. Addiction specialists offer several theories for this extraordinarily high prevalence, one of which is tremendous pressure on young people to be successful from the time they are small children. They often spend what little free time they have getting lost in the virtual world of role-playing games. Von Deneen explains: "Americans don't have a lot of personal time, but Chinese seem to have even less. They work 12 hours a day, six days a week. They work very, very hard. Sometimes the Internet is their greatest and only escape."[21]

A boy who spent four straight days in an Internet café in China receives an intravenous drip at a hospital whose focus is treating Internet addicts. China considers online addiction to be a serious public health issue, particularly among the nation's youth.

Can People Recover from Online Addiction?

Online addiction specialists say that the most challenging issue related to treatment is breaking through the addict's denial that he or she has a problem. Says Young: "Similar to alcoholism, the Internet addict must first realize the addiction and be motivated to seek help."[22] Yet even those who acknowledge their problem and are motivated to overcome it often face the difficulty of finding professionals who can help them, because treatment options are scarce in the United States. This is starting to change, however. A growing number of health-care facilities—including McLean Hospital, a psychiatric facility affiliated with Harvard Medical School, and the Illinois Institute for Addiction Recovery—are adding Internet addiction to the disorders they treat. In August 2009 a program known as reSTART opened in Fall City, Washington, and became America's first inpatient treatment center for Internet addiction.

Some Asian countries are far ahead of the United States in providing treatment for online addiction. To combat the problem in South Korea, for instance, the government has opened approximately 200 counseling centers and hospitals and has trained over 1,000 professional counselors to treat the disorder. One facility is the Save the Brain Clinic, which is located in Gongju, South Korea. The center offers a five-week treatment regimen for Internet addicts, who participate in group therapy sessions and art therapy. Patients also undergo transcranial magnetic stimulation, a procedure that uses magnetic fields to stimulate nerve cells in the brain and has been successful in treating depression and other disorders.

Concern and Controversy

Since the web opened the Internet to the world in the 1990s, the online population has grown exponentially. In countless ways this has been positive, with features and applications that have changed how people communicate, conduct business, shop, socialize, and play. Yet along with the phenomenal advantages offered by the Internet, a new type of addiction has emerged. Many specialists believe online addiction is just as serious as alcoholism and drug addiction, whereas others reject this idea. In the coming years more cases of online addiction will undoubtedly be reported—but whether the controversy will be resolved is unknown.

Is Online Addiction Real?

> **Is internet addiction real? I think it is real for the people who experience it. I think it is real for the people who describe their lives as out of control due to their compulsive behaviors involving the internet.**
>
> —DeeAnna Merz Nagel, a clinical counselor and cofounder of the Online Therapy Institute in Highlands, New Jersey.

> **The growing use of the Internet in everyday life has raised concerns that large numbers of people have become 'Internet addicts' and that the Internet is dehumanizing us. Despite the credibility of some of the people who raise these concerns, the evidence is anything but conclusive.**
>
> —Michael Friedman, an adjunct associate professor at the Columbia University Schools of Social Work and Public Health.

In 1995, when New York psychiatrist Ivan Goldberg coined the phrase "Internet addiction disorder," he was playing a trick on the mental health professionals who frequented his online group PsyCom.net. Introducing the new "illness" was Goldberg's way of poking fun at the APA for characterizing virtually all unusual behaviors as addictions. He even fabricated a group of symptoms, which included anxiety, obsessive thinking about what was happening on the Internet, fantasizing and dreaming about the Internet, and "voluntary or involuntary typing movements of the fingers."[23] Goldberg then set up an online support forum called the Internet Addiction Support Group and invited people to participate.

The humor in what he had done was obvious to Goldberg—but what happened afterward made it clear that not everyone got the joke. He received an onslaught of e-mails from people who confided about their Internet-related problems, and post after post appeared on the forum. Journalist David Wallis wrote about this in a 1997 *New Yorker* article:

> Word of the group spread faster than a computer virus. Hundreds of self-described addicts—some claiming to surf the Net twelve hours a day posted their pain. "I did have a RL (real life) prior to this 'electronic take-over,'" one user bemoaned. "My computer's keyboard has worn off after less than a year." Another confessed, "I've been thinking of getting a second home phone installed in order to be able to talk to my family once in a while."[24]

Identifying a Problem

A year before Goldberg publicized his spoof of Internet addiction, psychologist Kimberly S. Young was taking a serious look at what she perceived as a growing problem. After hearing about people whose lives were negatively affected by their incessant online activities, Young became concerned. She found one case to be especially disturbing. It involved a woman in her early forties, with no prior addiction or psychiatric history, who had been happy and content with her family and home life. The woman, who described herself as computer illiterate, had joined America Online and found it surprisingly easy to navigate—so much so that the time she spent in chat rooms quickly grew from a few hours a week to up to 60 hours a week.

The woman felt excited whenever she was participating in virtual communities, whereas being offline left her feeling depressed, anxious, and irritable. To avoid these feelings of withdrawal, which she likened to being an alcoholic without alcohol, she rearranged her schedule to make time on the Internet her highest priority. In the first case history of online addiction that was ever published, Young wrote: "The subject canceled appointments, stopped calling real life friends, reduced her interpersonal involvement with her family, and quit social activities she once enjoyed, e.g., bridge club. Further, she stopped performing routine chores, such as the cooking, cleaning, and grocery shopping, that would take her away from being on-line."[25] Within one year of purchasing her home computer, the woman's life had fallen apart. Her husband of 17 years left her, and she had little or no interaction with her two teenage daughters.

Because of this and other similar cases, Young became dedicated to the study of Internet addiction. Her 1998 *Caught in the Net* was the first book to identify it as a real disorder and offer hope to those who were affected by it. She also issued a warning about the Internet, which at the time had only a fraction of the users that are online today: "We're bombarded with cultural messages that urge us to welcome this new tool, and we're assured that it will only improve and enrich our lives. It has that capability. But it also has an addictive potential with harmful consequences that, left undetected and unchecked, could silently run rampant in our schools, our universities, our offices, our libraries, and our homes."[26]

> In 1995, when New York psychiatrist Ivan Goldberg coined the phrase "Internet addiction disorder," he was playing a trick on the mental health professionals who frequented his online group PsyCom.net.

In the months following the release of *Caught in the Net*, Young was stunned by the response from people all over the world. She explains: "I heard from parents, spouses, and addicts themselves struggling to deal with an addiction that they could not understand."[27] According to Young, her book offered these people understanding and validation of what they were going through and gave credence to a disorder that many clinicians either knew nothing about or scoffed at. Before long, other mental health professionals reported seeing patients who suffered from Internet-related disorders, and this led to increased recognition of the problem. Awareness of online addiction continued to grow as numerous books and research papers were published, and mental health facilities began to add compulsive Internet use to the addiction disorders they treated.

Changing Views on Addiction

The online addiction controversy has many facets. Some mental health professionals argue that the Internet can be every bit as addictive as chemical substances, while others reject the notion that someone can actually be addicted to a behavior or activity. This difference of opinion is not surprising, considering that addiction itself has been a topic of debate for decades. Prior to the nineteenth century, for example, the prevailing belief about alcohol and drugs was that desire, rather than irresistible urges or cravings, led people to use them. As the years went by, this viewpoint began to change, and addiction was widely recognized as a serious problem. Exactly what it was and what caused it, however, continued to be debated.

> The online addiction controversy has many facets. Some mental health professionals argue that the Internet can be every bit as addictive as chemical substances, while others reject the notion that someone can actually be addicted to a behavior or activity.

In 1957 the World Health Organization (WHO) issued a formal definition of addiction, calling it a "state of periodic or chronic intoxication produced by repeated consumption of a drug (natural or synthetic)."[28] Characteristics of addiction included an overpowering compulsion (desire or need) to continue taking the drug and to obtain it by any means, a tendency to need increasing amounts, a psychological and physical dependence on the drug's effects, and a detrimental effect on the individual and society.

In the years since the WHO formally defined addiction, research has yielded a great deal of information about how and why addiction occurs. Today the predominant belief among scientists is that it is a brain disorder that originates in a region known as the mesolimbic pathway, which controls pleasure and reward through a chemical known as dopamine. Once someone has experienced the pleasant effects of a dopamine rush, he or she feels compelled to repeat certain actions in pursuit of the same effects again. Recent studies have suggested that this not only applies to the ingesting of alcohol or drugs, but also to behaviors such as compulsive Internet use.

Although the viewpoint that addiction also applies to behaviors is controversial, it has been embraced by many experts and psychiatric organizations, including the American Society of Addiction Medicine (ASAM). Long known for its position that addiction was solely related to substance abuse, the group changed its stance on the basis of research by top addiction experts, addiction medicine specialists, and leading neuroscience researchers. In a February 2012 news release, the ASAM states: "Internet addiction has not been formally accepted as a psychiatric diagnosis. However, it has many features in common with other addictive diseases."[29] Like other addictions, the group says that Internet addiction involves a compulsive need, lack of related control over the behavior, and disregard for adverse consequences.

The DSM Debate

When the APA first announced that Internet addiction was being considered for inclusion in the revised DSM, Young and other experts saw this as an encouraging development. For years they had lobbied for it, believing that a distinct diagnostic category would increase credibility and acceptance of online addiction among mental health professionals, which would, in turn, lead to better care for sufferers. In February 2010, however, supporters of the measure were disappointed to learn that the DSM-V working group had ruled against it. Nora Volkow, who is director of the National Institute on Drug Abuse and a member of the group, explains the rationale behind the decision: "In order to include something in DSM-V, there needs to be sufficient scientific evidence about the importance and credibility of the particular disorder. That type of information as it pertains to the U.S. is not there for Internet addiction."[30]

A number of mental health professionals approved of the APA's decision. They have different reasons for objecting to Internet addiction's

> " Although the viewpoint that addiction also applies to behaviors is controversial, it has been embraced by many experts and psychiatric organizations, including the American Society of Addiction Medicine. "

being included in the DSM, one of which is skepticism that it is a real disorder. This is the perspective of New York psychologist Todd Essig, who says that designating it as a mental illness takes the focus away from personal responsibility and the freedom to make choices. Also, says Essig, including Internet addiction in the DSM would have been a bad move because it "opens the diagnostic door" to every conceivable problem, from getting too many tattoos to newspaper hoarding, overeating, and "whatever else comes along."[31]

Symptoms of a Deeper Problem?

Many who reject that compulsive online behavior is an addiction contend that it is probably a symptom of a larger problem. Ronald Pies, a professor of psychiatry at State University of New York Upstate Medical University, explains: "From what we know, many so-called 'Internet addicts' are folks who have severe depression, anxiety disorders, or social phobic symptoms that make it hard for them to live a full, balanced life and deal face-to-face with other people. It may be that unless we treat their underlying problems, some new form of 'addiction' will pop up down the line."[32]

Colin Drummond, a psychiatrist with King's College in the United Kingdom, shares Pies's perspective. Drummond agrees that compulsive Internet use can be a serious problem but says that does not necessarily indicate addictive behavior. He explains: "If people have emotional problems and that leads them to use the internet obsessively then they obviously need help to deal with those problems, but that's quite different [from] saying that the internet is addictive." In Drummond's opinion, mental health practitioners need to look for the root cause of problematic Internet use, rather than assuming that it *is* the disorder. "They are treating an addiction rather than emotional problems that might lead to the emotional behaviour," he says. "Excessive internet use is a symptom, not a cause of a person's problems."[33]

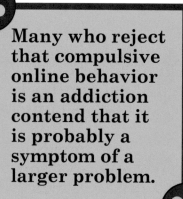

" Many who reject that compulsive online behavior is an addiction contend that it is probably a symptom of a larger problem. "

A study published in January 2012 seems to contradict this perspective. Researchers concluded that online addiction is a real disorder and that it causes alterations in the brain that affect whether addicts can kick their habit. Conducted by a research team from China, the study involved 33 adolescents, 17 of whom had been diagnosed with Internet addiction disorder. The team used magnetic resonance imaging technology to scan the young people's brains, and then compared the results of the two groups. In the scans of the addicted teens, the researchers could see visible abnormalities in white matter, which is the part of the brain that contains nerve cells and facilitates rapid-fire communication between them. This was a profound discovery because prior studies have shown similar effects in the brains of patients addicted to alcohol, cocaine, and other drugs.

The researchers were optimistic about the study's finding. They acknowledge, however, that there is no way to know whether the brain impairment happened as a result of Internet addiction or if it already existed and made the young people more prone to becoming addicted. Says Jonathan Wallis, an associate professor of psychology and neuroscience at the University of California–Berkeley who is familiar with the Chinese study: "We don't know whether the poor insulation connecting these areas of the brain predisposes these people to developing compulsive behaviors or whether engaging in a behavior repetitively could damage the connections between brain areas."[34]

Much Left to Learn

Online addiction is a relatively new phenomenon, having been identified less than two decades ago. Yet it is already a source of controversy among mental health professionals, with some convinced that it is a serious disorder while others argue that it is a symptom of some other disorder. Despite the difference in viewpoints, most experts agree that further study is needed. Young writes: "Overall, I can say that we are only beginning to understand the impact of the Internet. It is my hope that in the next decade we will understand so much more about its social and clinical implications."[35]

Primary Source Quotes*

Is Online Addiction Real?

Primary Source Quotes

* Editor's Note: While the definition of a primary source can be narrowly or broadly defined, for the purposes of Compact Research, a primary source consists of: 1) results of original research presented by an organization or researcher; 2) eyewitness accounts of events, personal experience, or work experience; 3) first-person editorials offering pundits' opinions; 4) government officials presenting political plans and/or policies; 5) representatives of organizations presenting testimony or policy.

> ❝DSM-V proposes to incorporate *some* non-substance addictions—notably gambling. (Internet addiction is still up in the air—will the Task Force decide if it is addictive by a PET scan or by majority vote?)❞

—Stanton Peele, "War over Addiction: Evaluating the DSM-V," Stanton Peele Addiction Website, February 11, 2010. http://peele.net.

Peele is a psychologist, attorney, addiction expert, and author.

> ❝What is it about this modern invention that crosses the line from entertainment and simple utility to an addiction that can cost people their jobs, their shelter, and even their health?❞

—Winston Ross, "A World Wide Woe," Daily Beast, October 7, 2009. www.thedailybeast.com.

Ross is a journalist from Eugene, Oregon, who says that Internet addiction is the reason his brother has been homeless for most of his adult life.

> ❝What most people online who think they are addicted are probably suffering from is the desire to not want to deal with other problems in their lives.❞

—John M. Grohol, "Internet Addiction Guide," Psych Central, January 5, 2012. http://psychcentral.com.

Grohol is a psychologist and the publisher of the Psych Central website.

> ❝The concept of Internet addiction was socially constructed before substantial scientific or clinical research had been performed.❞

—Timothy Liu and Marc N. Potenza, "Problematic Internet Use: Clinical Aspects," in *Impulse Control Disorders*, ed. Elias Aboujaoude and Lorrin M. Koran. New York: Cambridge University Press, 2010.

Liu and Potenza are with the Department of Psychiatry at Yale University School of Medicine.

66 It would appear that if Internet addiction does indeed exist, it affects only a relatively small percentage of the online population and there is very little evidence that it is problematic among adolescents. 99

—Robert Zheng, Jason Burrow-Sanchez, and Clifford Drew, eds., *Adolescent Online Social Communication and Behavior.* Hershey, PA: Information Science Reference, 2010.

Zheng, Burrow-Sanchez, and Drew are psychologists with the University of Utah.

66 Research is only now beginning to determine which youth may be at most risk for online addiction. 99

—Shu-Sha Angie Guan and Kaveri Subrahmanyam, "Youth Internet Use: Risks and Opportunities," Medscape Today, June 25, 2009. www.medscape.com.

Guan is a researcher for the Children's Digital Media Center in Los Angeles, and Subrahmanyam is the group's associate director.

66 While most people use the Internet daily with little problem, using the Internet becomes the top priority in the lives of addicts. 99

—Howard Padwa and Jacob Cunningham, eds., *Addiction: A Reference Encyclopedia.* Santa Barbara, CA: Greenwood, 2010.

Padwa is a public policy researcher, and Cunningham teaches history at Hebrew Union College in Los Angeles.

Is Online Addiction Real?

- According to Elias Aboujaoude's 2011 book *Virtually You*, Internet addiction prevalence ranges from **0.3 percent** (from a US population survey) to nearly **38 percent** in a study of teens and young adults in Hong Kong.

- In a 2010 study of college students conducted by researchers from Melbourne, Australia, about **10 percent** were found to be in the at-risk category for Internet addiction.

- A 2011 study by Dimitri A. Christakis and colleagues found a link between problematic Internet use and moderate to severe **depression** among college students.

- A 2009 study, which involved 1,618 teenagers from Guangdong Province in China, found that teens who were severely addicted to the Internet were nearly **5 times** more likely to have intentionally injured themselves in the past 6 months.

- A 2011 study of 3,560 high school students in Connecticut found that problematic Internet use was most common among Asian (**7.86 percent**) and Hispanic (**6.07 percent**) teens.

- According to psychologist Kimberly S. Young, research has shown that over **50 percent** of those with Internet addiction also suffer from other addictions, such as: alcohol, drugs, or nicotine.

Risk Factors for Online Addiction

Online addiction experts have identified characteristics commonly seen in people who become addicted to Internet activities. Some mix of these characteristics might put a person at risk for an addiction to online activities, according to a 2010 paper by an Indian psychiatrist.

Gender/Age	Male
	College student
	Adolescent or young adult
Personality traits	Shyness
	Low self-esteem
	Poor emotional and social skills
	Tendency toward risk-taking behavior
	Becomes easily bored
	Sensation seeking
	Poor time-management skills
	Introverted in face-to-face interactions
	Loneliness
	Negative coping styles (retreats into fantasy rather than approaching and solving problems rationally)
Family factors	Parental separation
	Parental overprotection
	Raised in hierarchical, family-focused societies (such as in South Korea)
	Observations of online social network use by parents and friends

Source: Shahul Ameen, "Internet Addiction: A Review," Centre for Addiction Recovery, September 2010. www.deaddiction.co.uk.

Characteristics of Online Addiction in College Students

Adolescents and young adults have been shown to be at high risk for developing online addictions. A study conducted by researchers in Washington and Wisconsin between September 2009 and August 2010 found that 4 percent of college students who participated in the study had some level of problematic attachment to the Internet. Many of these students experienced common symptoms of addiction, including a negative effect on schoolwork and grades, and loss of sleep becauseof online activity.

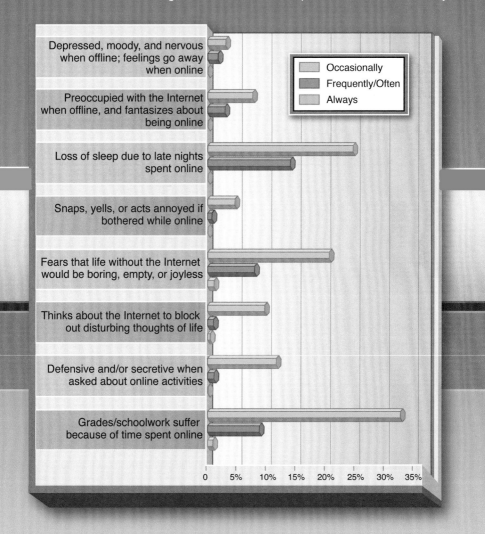

Note: Scale only goes up to 35 percent.

Source: Dimitri A. Christakis et al., "Problematic Internet Usage in US College Students: A Pilot Study," *BMC Medicine*, 2011. www.biomedcentral.com.

Disorder or Symptom of Mental Illness?

Not all mental health professionals consider excessive Internet use to be a sign of addiction. Some believe it to be a symptom of other problems such as depression or attention-deficit/hyperactivity disorder (ADHD). To examine this connection, researchers from Taiwan performed a study of more than 2,000 middle school students and found that most who had been diagnosed with Internet addiction also suffered from another mental health disorder. The team concluded that these mental illnesses could increase the risk for addictive behavior, rather than online addiction being the disorder itself.

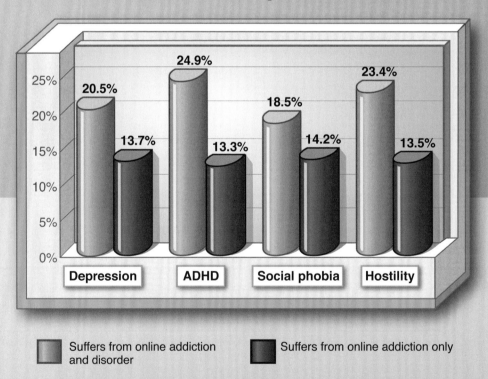

Of those classified as having Internet addiction . . .

Depression: 20.5% / 13.7%
ADHD: 24.9% / 13.3%
Social phobia: 18.5% / 14.2%
Hostility: 23.4% / 13.5%

Suffers from online addiction and disorder

Suffers from online addiction only

Note: Scale only goes up to 25 percent.

Source: Chih-Hung Ko et al., "Predictive Values of Psychiatric Symptoms for Internet Addiction in Adolescents," *Archives of Pediatrics & Adolescent Medicine*, October 2009. http://archpedi.ama-assn.org.

People Admit to Internet Addiction

A January 2012 article on the news website Mashable provided highlights of an Internet addiction study, and readers were invited to share comments about their own Internet-related behavior. Over 6,000 people participated in the online poll and as this chart shows, over 30 percent were either positive or fairly certain that they had an Internet addiction.

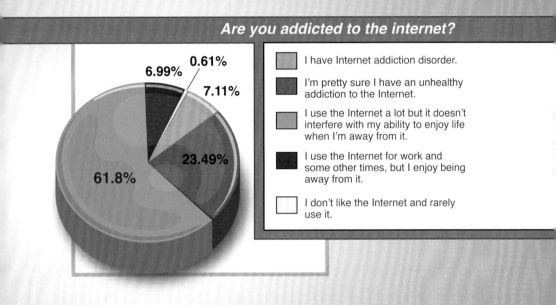

Are you addicted to the internet?

0.61% — I have Internet addiction disorder.

6.99% — I'm pretty sure I have an unhealthy addiction to the Internet.

7.11% — I use the Internet a lot but it doesn't interfere with my ability to enjoy life when I'm away from it.

23.49% — I use the Internet for work and some other times, but I enjoy being away from it.

61.8% — I don't like the Internet and rarely use it.

Source: Kate Freeman, "Internet Overuse Could Cause Structural Brain Damage," *Mashable*, January 13, 2012. www.mashable.com.

- A January 2010 report by researchers from Shaanxi, China, revealed that an estimated **7 percent** of Chinese elementary and middle school students suffer from Internet addiction, with the frequency among males being more than twice that of females.

- A 2010 study by researchers Lawrence T. Lam and Zi-Wen Peng found that the risk of depression for pathological Internet users was **2.5 times** higher than for those who did not use the Internet excessively.

- In a 2011 study by Dimitri A. Christakis and colleagues, **30 percent** of respondents said they often stayed online longer than intended, and **10 percent** said this was always the case.

Can People Get Addicted to Social Networking?

"Just a decade ago, it was noted that there was indeed an Internet addiction, but with the explosion of sites such as Twitter and especially the heavyweight champ, Facebook, we can now add addiction to social networking sites to the list."

—Dale Archer, a psychiatrist from Lake Charles, Louisiana.

"Does the fact that we're now socializing with the help of some technology . . . change the basic process of socialization? Perhaps, a bit. But not so significantly as to warrant a disorder."

—John M. Grohol, a psychologist and publisher of the Psych Central website.

A college student named April is convinced that online social networking is addictive because of what she has personally experienced. Whenever she sits down at the computer to work on a task, such as writing an essay, it takes her an hour to even get started, as she explains: "'Just one quick look at Facebook,' I think to myself. I then end up on the website for an extended period of time." April believes her inability to concentrate is a sign of how addictive social networking can be. "Social media is like a drug," she says. "There's a euphoric high that comes from having a new notification or post, like the high from a snort of cocaine or smoke of marijuana."[36]

The obvious solution is to just pull the plug, but April says this is much harder than it sounds. "Like any other drug, it takes over the daily lives of its users and is extremely difficult to quit using," she says. "The lows of not being able to [get online] when they want is like the draw of an addictive drug and the painful withdrawals of not knowing what is going on are just like the withdrawals of a druggie after quitting. Whatever the poison, it takes over the students' lives."[37]

"Facebook Addiction Disorder"

The theory that online and drug addictions are more alike than different was one finding of a study by British researchers Daria J. Kuss and Mark D. Griffiths. Published in August 2011, it involved an in-depth analysis of psychological literature and research conducted between 1996 and 2011. The authors' intent was to better understand why people are so drawn to social networking, examine the personalities of users, evaluate their usage patterns, determine the positive and negative effects of social networking, and explore the potential for addiction. During their investigation, Kuss and Griffiths learned that the time people spend on Facebook increased nearly 600 percent from 2007 to 2008. They write: "This statistic alone indicates the exponential appeal of SNSs [social networking sites] and also suggests a reason for a rise in potential SNS addiction. . . . From a clinical psychologist's perspective, it may be plausible to speak specifically of 'Facebook Addiction Disorder.'"[38]

> The theory that online and drug addictions are more alike than different was one finding of a study by British researchers Daria J. Kuss and Mark D. Griffiths.

Kuss and Griffiths concluded that social networking addiction resembles chemical addiction in a number of ways. Both involve an attempt to escape from reality, mental and emotional preoccupation, and mood-modifying experiences, and both typically result in neglect of one's personal life and conflict with friends and loved ones. Also, both types of addicts attempt to conceal their unhealthy behavior and eventually develop a tolerance for it, meaning that over time they need more and more to achieve the desired effects. Another finding was that like substance abusers, social networking addicts suffer from withdrawal symptoms when they cannot be online, and they have a high rate of relapse, whereby they revert back to their excessive online activity after a period of abstinence.

To illustrate how closely social networking addiction resembles substance addiction, the 2011 study cites the case of a 24-year-old woman whose dependence on social networking significantly interfered with her life. Kuss and Griffiths write:

> She used Facebook excessively for at least five hours a day and was dismissed from her job because she continuously checked her SNS instead of working. Even during the clinical interview, she used her mobile phone to access Facebook. In addition to excessive use that led to significant impairment in a variety of areas in the woman's life, she developed anxiety symptoms as well as insomnia.[39]

An Irresistible Pull

From the time that social networking sites were first launched, they have been extremely popular, and they will undoubtedly become even more so in the future. Facebook, Tumblr, YouTube, Twitter, and other online services offer numerous advantages to users and can be fun, entertaining, and enlightening. But when social networking begins to dominate someone's life, he or she may be at risk for addiction. Kuss and Griffiths offer an example: "'*I'm an addict. I just get lost in Facebook.*' replies a young mother when asked why she does not see herself able to help her daughter with her homework. Instead of supporting her child, she spends her time chatting and browsing the social network site. This case, while extreme, is suggestive of a potential new mental health problem that emerges as Internet social networks proliferate."[40]

Although not all mental health professionals agree, those who specialize in online addiction warn that the irresistible allure of social networking can lead to obsession. The addiction treatment group Elements Behavioral Health refers to the millions of people who are so hooked on social networking that they tune in whether they are at a desk in front of a computer, walking down the street, driving in a car, or sitting in a classroom. The group writes: "Despite claims of the benefits of being constantly in touch with friends, such slavish devotion to social networking sites can quickly lead to addiction."[41]

According to Elements Behavioral Health, a number of warning signs can reveal that someone is addicted to social networking. The first, and most obvious, is that he or she cannot function in everyday life without being able to get online. Other symptoms include spending excessive time online; ignoring responsibilities at home, work, or school; and the inability to sleep, as the group writes: "Staying up all night (or the better part of it), trying to connect and write your most clever thoughts on your Wall, will really eat into your energy level. You'll find yourself dragging through the next day, unable to concentrate on whatever it is you're supposed to be doing—not a good thing, and certainly not conducive to overall mental and/or physical well-being."[42]

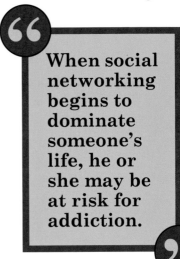

When social networking begins to dominate someone's life, he or she may be at risk for addiction.

A Revealing Study

Online addiction experts agree that the most obvious sign of problematic social networking use is excessive time devoted to it, along with how difficult it is for some users to disconnect. This was one finding of a March 2010 study by the consumer electronics group Retrevo, which involved interviews with 1,000 adults in the United States. The study revealed that 48 percent of respondents updated and/or read Facebook or Twitter anytime they woke up during the night and as soon as they got up in the morning, with 28 percent of iPhone users saying they hopped online even before they were out of bed. A number of participants viewed Facebook and Twitter as such a high priority that they saw no problem with interrupting dinner, trips to the bathroom, or romantic encounters in order to check for messages or status updates.

When the survey was complete, Retrevo executive Andrew Eisner observed in a blog post that many people appear to be obsessed with constantly exchanging information with their friends, family, and coworkers. He was concerned over some of the study findings, as he explains: "We're not qualified to declare a societal, social media crisis, but when almost half of social media users say they check Facebook or Twitter sometime during the night or when they first wake up, you have to wonder if these people aren't suffering from some sort of addiction to social media."[43]

Tempting Tweets

Twitter is a real-time social networking service that affords users a non-stop stream of commentary, opinions, and the latest news, based on their individual preferences and what they want to hear about. Twitter updates, known as tweets, are short bursts of information that are no more than 140 characters and can include photos and videos as well as text. The popularity of Twitter has skyrocketed since it was first introduced—as of 2012 there were 500 million registered users—and the number continues to climb each day. As with all types of social networking, most people who use Twitter are able to balance it with their other hobbies and interests and do not use it excessively. For some, however, Twitter has become so irresistible that they cannot stay away from it, meaning that tweeting (and reading tweets) has become an obsession.

> Online addiction experts agree that the most obvious sign of problematic social networking use is excessive time devoted to it, along with how difficult it is for some users to disconnect.

This is what happened to Laurel Snyder, an author of children's books who lives in Atlanta, Georgia. When she first signed on to Twitter, Snyder was not particularly fond of it because she did not understand how it worked. Before long, though, she became a huge fan—so much so that it started to monopolize her time. "I was OK with e-mail and Facebook," she says. "But Twitter! Twitter is different. It's faster and bigger and looser. It's the biggest cocktail party in the world, 24-7."[44] Snyder began to rely on Twitter for news, entertainment, connections to friends, and the latest updates from people she admires. This was all available to her anytime she felt like tuning in, as she writes:

> Twitter never goes to bed. Twitter is useful. Twitter is good. Twitter is too good. I have, at my fingertips, the world I have sought all my life. I can eavesdrop on conversations between editors. I can send messages to Bruce Springsteen. Stalk ex-boyfriends. Who wants to walk away from that? Why does anyone ever leave the house? Well, um, because meanwhile—my kids are watching TV, the dishes are piling up, my new book is behind schedule. I haven't showered. And I haven't even noticed. I'm too busy to notice.[45]

Although Snyder realized that she was spending far too much time on Twitter, she was not aware of how much she depended on it until the service was offline for a day. That morning she sat in front of her computer, started to launch Twitter, and was dismayed to find that the site was down. Panic quickly set in, as she writes: "Actually, it was funny, in a kind of pathetic, soul-crushing way: I stared at the blank screen, hitting refresh over and over. Waiting for everyone to come back. For my online life to resume. Finally, I accepted the truth. Twitter, my favorite unreliable news source and constant companion, was gone."[46]

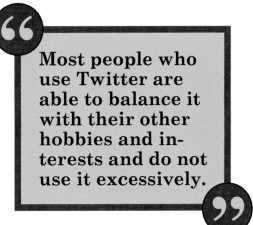

Most people who use Twitter are able to balance it with their other hobbies and interests and do not use it excessively.

Snyder forced herself to walk away from the computer, go outside, and enjoy the sunshine. Throughout the day she tried not to think about Twitter but found that to be impossible. "Wherever I went," she says, "I took Twitter with me. I was *thinking* in Twitter! All afternoon, my mind percolated with 140-character thoughts that I longed to share with anyone. No, with *everyone*."[47]

Facing the severity of her problem was disturbing to Snyder, as well as frightening, and she vowed to overcome her addiction. She stayed offline for a few days, but it was tough. "In the morning," she writes, "my need to touch the computer was nearly overpowering." Over time, Snyder has managed to limit her online time to no more than an hour each day. She has made progress, but is not convinced that she is totally cured. "Each time I post," she says, "I slam the computer shut with a *wham!* Each time it's like I'm testing myself. Because with Twitter and me, the minute it feels too natural, the minute it feels like a real conversation, is the minute I start to worry."[48]

Love It, Hate It

Online social networking offers numerous benefits to users, from easily connecting with friends and family to staying on top of the latest news from around the world. It can become a problem for those who develop an obsession with it, but whether this means they are addicted is a source of controversy among mental health professionals. A growing number, however, are starting to recognize it as a problem that needs to be taken seriously.

Primary Source Quotes*

Can People Get Addicted to Social Networking?

66 Can social media networking become an addiction if left unchecked? The answer, my friends, is yes. 99

—Gregory Jantz, "Today on CNN Headline News: My Thoughts on Social Media Addiction," A Place of Hope, January 8, 2010. www.aplaceofhope.com.

Jantz is a psychologist and founder of the mental health–care center A Place of Hope in Seattle, Washington.

66 To date, the scientific literature addressing the addictive qualities of social networks on the Internet is scarce. 99

— Daria J. Kuss and Mark D. Griffiths, "Online Social Networking and Addiction—a Review of the Psychological Literature," *International Journal of Environmental Research and Public Health*, August 29, 2011. www.mdpi.com.

Both from the United Kingdom, Kuss is a doctoral researcher in the area of online addiction, and Griffiths is a psychologist and gambling addiction expert.

Primary Source Quotes

❝Can we become addicted to Facebook? I think the answer is yes. While Facebook is not a mood or mind-altering substance (like alcohol or drugs), its overuse can cause 'clinically significant impairment or distress.'❞

—Stephanie Smith, "Addicted to Facebook?," Dr. Stephanie, May 27, 2011. www.drstephaniesmith.com.

Smith is a psychologist who is a co-owner of a group practice in Erie, Colorado.

❝I posted every hour on the hour, day and night, using a Web site that enabled me to tweet while asleep. It was an obsession. And like most obsessions, no good came of it.❞

—Larry Carlat, "Confessions of a Tweeter," *New York Times*," November 11, 2011. www.nytimes.com.

Carlat is a writer, editor, and web professional from New York City who says he became seriously addicted to Twitter.

❝There has been a little flurry of news articles and blogs recently about social media addiction. First of all, it concerns me that, as a society, we are very cavalier tossing around the concept of 'addiction.' Addiction is a serious psychological diagnosis based on specific and seriously life-impairing criteria.❞

—Pamela Brown Rutledge, "Social Media Addiction: Engage Brain Before Believing," *Psychology Today*, May 22, 2010. www.psychologytoday.com.

Rutledge is director of the Media Psychology Research Center in Palo Alto, California.

❝Across the country, students are constantly distracted by an addiction to social media. These websites prevent successful learning and are emotionally destructive to users.❞

—April H., "Teens on Facebook: When Does It Become Too Much?," *Huffington Post*, November 11, 2011. www.huffingtonpost.com.

April H. is a teenage girl from Peoria, Arizona.

66 Individuals who suffer from an addiction to chat rooms, IM, or social networking sites become over-involved in online relationships or may engage in virtual adultery. Online friends quickly become more important to the individual often at the expense of real life relationships with family and friends. 99

—Kimberly S. Young, "What Is Internet Addiction?," HealthyPlace, January 12, 2012. www.healthyplace.com.

Young is a psychologist, the director of the Center for Internet Addiction, and an expert in online addiction.

66 My antisocial behavior continued as my addictive energies turned from school to video games, and later to online social networking and chatting. I developed an addiction that kept me isolated from people. 99

—Kevin Roberts, "Confessions of a Cyber Junkie," *USA Today*, March 2011.

Roberts, who recovered from online addiction, conducts support groups for teens and adults who struggle with the same addiction.

66 Clearly, many, many kids spend way too much time in front of their computers and texting on cell phones—and much of that time is spent social networking. But it that all bad? The answer to that question is a big fat, 'Depends.' 99

—Wendy Walsh, "Is Your Teen Addicted to Social Media?," Mom Logic, June 28, 2010. www.momlogic.com.

Walsh is a psychologist from Los Angeles, California.

Can People Get Addicted to Social Networking?

- According to a 2011 report in the *International Journal of Environmental Research and Public Health*, the overall time spent on Facebook increased **566 percent** between 2007 and 2008.

- In a June 2011 survey by the online security firm Webroot that involved nearly 4,000 Internet users in the United States, United Kingdom, and Australia, **75 percent** of people between the ages of 18 and 34 said they felt addicted to social networking.

- In a February 2012 Fox News poll, **12.5 percent** of respondents said they were addicted to social networking.

- A study published in 2010 by University of New Hampshire professor Chuck Martin found no correlation between the **grades** students receive and the amount of time spent on sites such as Facebook or YouTube.

- As of 2012 over **500 groups** had been formed on Facebook for members to discuss their addiction to social networking.

- In a 2011 survey of parents in the United Kingdom, **80 percent** of respondents said they felt it was possible to become addicted to online social networking.

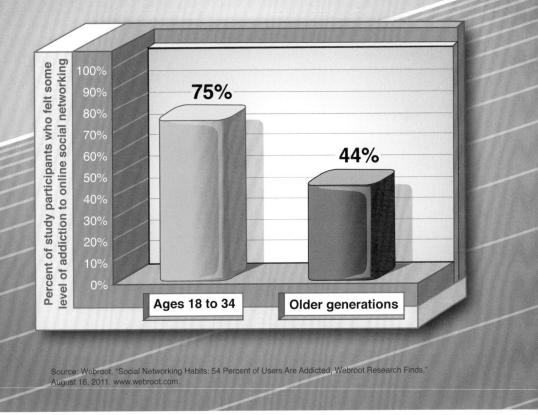

Over Half of Social Networking Users Addicted

During June 2011 the online security group Webroot asked nearly 4,000 Internet users in Australia, the United States, and the United Kingdom about their social networking habits. Over half of participants felt they had some level of addiction to their favorite social network, and as this chart shows, the highest percentage was between the ages of 18 and 34.

Percent of study participants who felt some level of addiction to online social networking

100%
90%
80%
70%
60%
50%
40%
30%
20%
10%
0%

75%

44%

Ages 18 to 34

Older generations

Source: Webroot, "Social Networking Habits: 54 Percent of Users Are Addicted, Webroot Research Finds," August 16, 2011. www.webroot.com.

- A report published in the April 2011 issue of the medical journal *Pediatrics* states that **22 percent** of teenagers log in to social networking sites more than 10 times a day.

- An August 2011 survey for Columbia University's National Center on Addiction and Substance Abuse found that only **30 percent** of 12- to 17-year-olds spend no time on social networking sites.

Many People Are Dependent on Social Networking

A 2010 study by the technology group Retrevo examined the habits of social networking users. Although it did not ask specifically whether people felt addicted, the behaviors they reported show that they are heavily dependent on Facebook and Twitter. As this graph shows, the heaviest social networking users were under age 25.

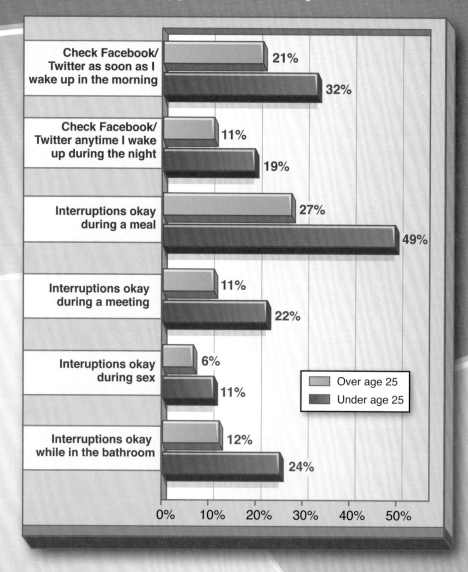

Check Facebook/Twitter as soon as I wake up in the morning: Over age 25 — 21%, Under age 25 — 32%

Check Facebook/Twitter anytime I wake up during the night: Over age 25 — 11%, Under age 25 — 19%

Interruptions okay during a meal: Over age 25 — 27%, Under age 25 — 49%

Interruptions okay during a meeting: Over age 25 — 11%, Under age 25 — 22%

Interuptions okay during sex: Over age 25 — 6%, Under age 25 — 11%

Interruptions okay while in the bathroom: Over age 25 — 12%, Under age 25 — 24%

Legend: Over age 25, Under age 25

*Note: Scale only goes up to 50 percent.

Source: Amy Porterfield, "Study Highlights Growing Social Media Addiction," Social Media Examiner, April 16, 2010. www.socialmediaexaminer.com.

Most People Think Social Networking Is Addictive

In February 2010 Fox News conducted an online poll and invited people to share their thoughts about social networking addiction. As this chart shows, over 66 percent of participants thought addiction was possible and nearly 13 percent admitted that they were addicted.

Can people develop drug-like addiction to social media sites?

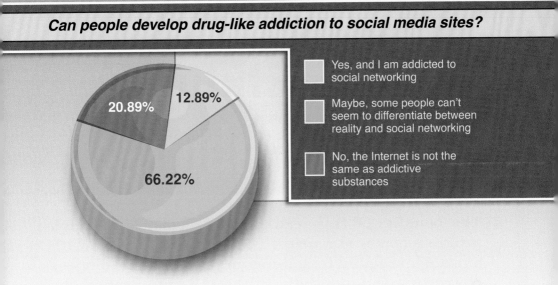

12.89% Yes, and I am addicted to social networking

20.89% Maybe, some people can't seem to differentiate between reality and social networking

66.22% No, the Internet is not the same as addictive substances

Source: Fox News, "Poll: Do You Think Social Networking Is More Addictive than Cigarettes or Alcohol?," February 7, 2012. http://foxnewsinsider.com.

- According to a February 2011 news release by Loyola University, over **80 percent** of divorce lawyers report that in recent years they have seen an increase in the number of divorce cases related to social networking.

- In a June 2011 survey by the online security firm Webroot that involved nearly 4,000 Internet users in the United States, United Kingdom, and Australia, **46 percent** of respondents said they visited their favorite social networks several times a day or constantly.

- A June 2010 paper by Elements Behavioral Health states that the primary symptom of addiction to online social networking is people's **inability to function** in everyday life without checking the sites at least once a day.

How Serious a Problem Is Compulsive Online Gaming and Gambling?

66 **The benefits of this technology are many; yet such progress comes at a price. The number of people with a problem related to gaming and use of other devices is growing exponentially in the U.S. and around the world.** 99

—Kevin Roberts, a former online gaming addict who now conducts support groups for teens and adults who struggle with the same addiction.

66 **In short, a gambling addict who uses the Internet to gamble is a gambling addict not an Internet addict. The Internet is just the place where they conduct their chosen (addictive) behavior.** 99

—Mark D. Griffiths, a psychologist and gambling addiction expert from the United Kingdom.

I n a February 2011 report, researchers from the United States and Singapore discuss the similarities between online gaming and gambling, saying that "the parallel seems justifiable."[49] Those whose passion is role-playing games, for example, are typically motivated by the excitement of winning, and the same is true of people who frequent Internet gambling sites. Also, getting lost in the virtual world for a while allows gamers and gamblers to relax and escape from their real-life concerns. For most individuals, this is not a problem. If they realize that they are spending too much time online, they take steps to cut back on Internet use. But for some, gaming or gambling becomes such a high priority that it significantly interferes with their lives, which could be a sign of addictive behavior. The authors of the 2011 report make it clear, however, that not all experts agree. "There is by no means a consensus on this issue," they write. "There still is heated debate about how best to define addictions, including behavioral addictions."[50]

Gaming Junkies

Kimberly S. Young is one expert who has no doubt about the addictive potential of online gaming and gambling. Young has observed that people who are addicted to these activities describe the "fix" of gaming or gambling in much the same way as substance abusers describe feeling about drugs. Referring to online gaming, she writes: "Gamers who become hooked show clear signs of addiction. Like a drug, gamers who play almost every day, play for extended periods of time (over 4 hours), get restless or irritable if they can't play, and sacrifice other social activities just to game are showing signs of addiction."[51]

Ben Alexander is painfully familiar with online gaming addiction because it once consumed his life. When he was a freshman at the University of Iowa, Alexander became obsessed with the role-playing game *World of Warcraft*. "At first," he says, "it was a couple of hours a day. By midway, through the first semester, I was playing 16 or 17 hours a day."[52] Previously someone who had spent hours each day reading, excelled in high school, and loved being a member of the school's cross-country team, Alexander lost interest in everything but the game. All he wanted to do was to be part of the online realm, where he equipped his characters with weaponry and conquered

> " Ben Alexander is painfully familiar with online gaming addiction because it once consumed his life.

his virtual enemies. He found his college studies boring because they did not challenge him like *World of Warcraft*, so he rarely went to class. Whenever he could not be on the computer, Alexander quickly grew frustrated and bored, and he spent his time plotting the moves he would make when he could get online again.

> According to reports by the South Korean government, an estimated 2 million citizens—nearly 1 in 10 users—suffer from Internet addiction, with most cases involving huge multiuser role-playing games.

By the second semester, Alexander was failing all his classes and dropped out of school. He confessed to his parents that he had a serious problem, and in a family session with a therapist, his mother offered an ultimatum: "It's hard for me to say this, but if you choose gaming, you will have to live on your own and support yourself."[53] The idea of giving up his most beloved activity seemed unbearable, but Alexander knew that he had no other choice. He voluntarily walked away from gaming and entered a specialized treatment program, with the goal of getting his life back together.

Crisis in South Korea

Studies have shown that online gaming addiction is especially severe in Asian countries, with one of the worst problems being in South Korea. Over 90 percent of the country's homes have high-speed Internet connections, compared with less than 70 percent in the United States. According to reports by the South Korean government, an estimated 2 million citizens—nearly 1 in 10 users—suffer from Internet addiction, with most cases involving huge multiuser role-playing games. Psychiatrist Kim Tae-hoon, who worries about the growing problem of gaming addiction in his country, shares his opinion about the root of it: "In South Korea it is easier for citizens to play online games than to invest in their offline personal relations through face-to-face conversations. People are becoming numb to human interaction."[54]

South Korean government authorities are most concerned about the proliferation of PC bangs, which are havens for online gaming fans. The country has about 22,000 of these establishments, which are open 24 hours a day, seven days a week. For a small hourly fee, gamers can spend as much time as they want getting lost in the virtual world. A man named Leon, who lives and teaches in South Korea, describes PC bangs as a "dream come true" for online gamers, as he writes:

> A PC Bang is a place where you go play, eat and relax in front of a 22 inch computer monitor on a puffy leather chair that will make you feel like a VIP. . . . The Internet connections at PC Bangs are usually lightning fast, the monitors big, and the computers modern and speedy. Combine this with a hazy, comfortable atmosphere and you'll soon realise why PC Bangs are one of the most popular forms of entertainment for most Koreans.[55]

> **Research specifically related to online gambling is scarce, so scientists are not certain whether it is more addictive than other types of gambling.**

Leon acknowledges, however, that even though PC bangs provide gamers with a place to relax and enjoy themselves, they are rife with potential for gaming addiction. "Korea has one of the highest addiction rates to online gaming," he says, "and stories of people neglecting real life in favour of playing some digital life they created for themselves in a game, is very sad, but very true. People have *actually died in PC Bangs* from a computer overdose (One guy played for three days straight, had a heart attack and it was suddenly game over)."[56] Other deaths have occurred in PC bangs as well. In December 2010 a 19-year-old South Korean man died after playing an online shooting game in a PC bang for 12 hours. He suddenly collapsed and was rushed to the hospital, but doctors were unable to save him.

"The Perfect Vehicle for Addiction"

Research specifically related to online gambling is scarce, so scientists are not certain whether it is more addictive than other types of gambling.

Although it is an issue of controversy, some addiction specialists insist that online gambling is worse. They argue that access at the click of a mouse is leading to an increase in gambling addiction, including among those who have not had gambling issues in the past. University of Connecticut psychologist Nancy Petry says that online gambling addiction resembles alcoholism. "It's similar to drinking—when you're developing a drinking problem you're doing it socially," says Petry, but she points out that many alcoholics eventually start drinking alone at home. Similarly, when people are gambling at home on a computer, "there are none of the social sanctions of real-world settings."[57] This, according to Petry, makes it more difficult for online gamblers to maintain control.

> " As the number of gambling websites has continued to grow, online addiction experts have observed an increase in addiction among people who never had gambling issues before. "

Josh Axelrad is convinced beyond any doubt that online gambling is the most addictive type of gambling, and he refers to it as "the perfect vehicle for addiction." Says Axelrad: "You never have to stop (you don't need to go home when you are home); it's private (your problems are easy to hide); and it plays at a riveting, breakneck speed. Casinos are a snore by comparison."[58] For five years Axelrad was a professional blackjack player, traveling to casinos all over the United States and netting over $700,000 for himself and a team of skilled friends. During the spring of 2005, he discovered online poker, and he says he was immediately hooked. Confident and smug because of his proven success at blackjack, he assumed that Internet gambling would be an easy way to make money—but he was wrong.

Axelrad thought nothing of betting $500 or $1,000 on one poker hand, but even when he kept losing, he could not stop gambling. At the time he was under contract to write a book, but he was so consumed with online poker that he could not focus on anything else. He writes:

> I would try to write, get stuck on my third or fourth sentence, log on to PartyPoker or Ultimate Bet, zap $500 or

a grand from my checking account to Gibraltar, and roll. I would bet. I would raise. I would raise. I would raise. . . . It was as if I were addicted. How ludicrous! You're a pro, I thought: get it together. Win back the 20 G's, please. Win back the 40 grand, if you would be so kind. I was staying awake for days straight, losing and gnashing my jaws. For months, I pressed on—for a year![59]

Axelrad eventually gambled away his entire $85,000 advance from the publisher and was so far behind on the book that he was in danger of losing the contract. This was his wake-up call, and it motivated him to give up Internet poker. Today he considers online gambling to be the most dangerous of all types of gambling, as he writes: "Most dangerous, you might ask? Surely online gambling is just clicking a mouse for a few bucks here and there, for giggles and to kill the odd hour? No. Internet wagering is—or has the potential to be—the most concentrated, most habit-engendering gambling environment known to humankind."[60]

A New Breed of Gambling Addicts?

As the number of gambling websites has continued to grow, online addiction experts have observed an increase in addiction among people who never had gambling issues before. This has been identified as a growing problem in the United Kingdom, where Internet gambling is becoming popular among women who would not be comfortable going alone to a casino. A January 2010 investigative story in the *Guardian* newspaper explains: "Evidence indicates that the number of women with [gambling] problems has doubled in recent years, and they now make up a quarter of addicts, although when it comes to online gambling the proportion is thought to be far higher. The explosion in internet gambling sites attracts more women than the traditionally male-dominated betting shops and casinos."[61]

According to Henrietta Bowden-Jones, who is a psychiatrist at the National Problem Gambling Clinic in London, England, it is not uncommon for women who discover the excitement of online gambling to play for 10 hours a day. She says that in an effort to hide their obsession with online gambling, these women often play while their partners are at work and shut down the computer before they come home.

This was the case with a British woman named Kath, who is married with two young sons. Once she became hooked on online gambling, she would drop the boys at school in the morning and return home to spend the entire day on gambling sites. The day never felt long enough, however. Kath became so immersed in gambling that she was consistently late in picking the boys up in the afternoon, and finally school officials confronted her. "The teacher called me in and said my youngest son was starting to get panicky around home time and that he had been crying when I was late," she says. "She was asking if there were any problems at home and I just felt irritated by her; I felt that she was interfering." As annoyed as Kath was, however, the reality of what she was doing to herself and her family was clear, and she realized that she had a serious problem. "All the anger turned to embarrassment, it all flooded over me," she says, "and I was shaking and crying. It was like an emotional cold turkey."[62]

Entertainment or Addiction?

For most people, online gaming and gambling are ways to relax, have fun, and spend a little while forgetting about normal day-to-day stress. Some, however, become dependent on their Internet activities at the expense of everything else, which online addiction specialists say is a clear sign that they have become addicted. Some experts disagree, arguing that the Internet is only the vehicle for a problem that already existed. But people like Ben Alexander, Kath, Josh Axelrad, and others who have lived through the trauma of addiction have no doubt that those experts are wrong.

Primary Source Quotes*

How Serious a Problem Is Compulsive Online Gaming and Gambling?

66 Compulsive gambling has been around for decades, but now access and opportunity are even greater with the invention of Internet gambling, bringing with it a new form of addictive behavior. 99

—Kimberly S. Young, "Online Gambling," Center for Internet Addiction, March 15, 2012. www.netaddiction.com.

Young is a psychologist, the director of the Center for Internet Addiction, and an expert in online addiction.

66 The case of Internet gambling provides little evidence that exposure is the primary driving force behind the prevalence and intensity of gambling. 99

—Howard J. Shaffer and Ryan Martin, "Disordered Gambling: Etiology, Trajectory and Clinical Considerations," *Annual Review of Clinical Psychiatry*, July 2011. http://thescholarship.ecu.edu.

Shaffer and Martin are professors at Harvard Medical School.

66 **For most adolescents, gaming is a pleasurable pastime activity. However, research suggests that excessive online gaming may in extreme cases lead to symptoms commonly experienced by substance addicts.** 99

—Daria J. Kuss and Mark D. Griffiths, "Adolescent Online Gaming Addiction," *Education and Health*, 2012.

Both from the United Kingdom, Kuss is a doctoral researcher in the area of online addiction, and Griffiths is a psychologist and gambling addiction expert.

66 **Like more traditional gambling addicts, people addicted to online gambling tend to hide their behaviors and feel a need to bet increasing amounts of money to gain emotional satisfaction from the experience.** 99

—Howard Padwa and Jacob Cunningham, eds., *Addiction: A Reference Encyclopedia*. Santa Barbara, CA: Greenwood, 2010.

Padwa is a public policy researcher, and Cunningham teaches history at Hebrew Union College in Los Angeles.

66 **In the same way that not all heavy gamers are addicts, not all negative outcomes associated with video gaming are addiction related.** 99

—Linda Criddle, "Not All Fun and Games—20-Year-Old Dies After Marathon Video Gaming Session," iLookBothWays, August 14, 2011. http://ilookbothways.com.

Criddle is an Internet safety and technology expert from Seattle, Washington.

66 **Online gambling constitutes a much greater risk of players becoming addicted than is the case with more conventional games of chance.** 99

—Laurent Beteille, *Promoting a Prevention Policy on Online Gambling Addiction*, report to the Social, Health and Family Affairs Committee, October 19, 2010. http://assembly.coe.int.

Beteille is a member of the Senate of France.

"Several researchers have begun testing scientifically the concept of pathological video game use, commonly called video game 'addiction.'"

—Douglas A. Gentile et al., "Pathological Video Game Use Among Youths: A Two-Year Longitudinal Study," *Pediatrics*, January 17, 2011. http://pediatrics.aappublications.org.

Gentile is with the Department of Psychology at Iowa State University.

"Major stories of addictive behavior generally come from multiplayer games, where gamers feel great responsibility for their own and their peers' success."

—Matthew Edlund, "Internet Gaming: The Latest Addiction," *Huffington Post*, March 11, 2011. www.huffingtonpost.com.

Edlund is a physician and director of the Center for Circadian Medicine in Sarasota, Florida.

"The popularity of video, computer, online, and virtual reality games has raised concern in both the popular media and the research community regarding the potential for negative health effects of gaming, including the potential for addiction."

—Rani A. Desai et al., "Video-Gaming Among High School Students: Health Correlates, Gender Differences, and Problematic Gaming," *Pediatrics*, November 15, 2010. http://pediatrics.aappublications.org.

The study authors are all with the Department of Psychology at Yale University School of Medicine.

How Serious a Problem Is Compulsive Online Gaming and Gambling?

- A study published in the Netherlands in 2010 found that online games, especially multiplayer role-playing games, were more often associated with **gaming addiction** than any other type of video game.

- According to British psychiatrist Henrietta Bowden-Jones, the majority of people who seek **psychiatric help** for serious Internet addiction are online gamers.

- In 1999 the Cato Institute reported that there were nearly 100 gambling sites on the web; by 2009 the American Gaming Association said the number had risen to more than **2,100**.

- The British Gambling Prevalence Survey, which was published in February 2011, found that the highest prevalence of pathological gamblers were those who gambled both online and offline.

- In a study published in 2009 by researchers Zaheer Hussain and Mark D. Griffiths, **41 percent** of online gamers acknowledged that they used gaming as an escape, and **7 percent** were classified as dependent on online gaming.

- According to a study published in April 2011 by Harvard Medical School professors Howard J. Shaffer and Ryan Martin, only **1 percent** of the US population has gambled online.

The Link Between Gaming Addiction and Unhealthy Behavior

To examine possible links between gaming addiction and risky or unhealthy behavior among teens, researchers from Yale University School of Medicine conducted a study of 4,028 high school students in Connecticut. Of those who fit the criteria* for problematic gaming, a high percentage smoked cigarettes or engaged in other risky behaviors.

Percent of online addicts who . . .

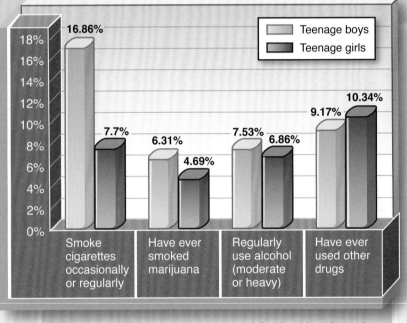

Legend:
- Teenage boys
- Teenage girls

	Teenage boys	Teenage girls
Smoke cigarettes occasionally or regularly	16.86%	7.7%
Have ever smoked marijuana	6.31%	4.69%
Regularly use alcohol (moderate or heavy)	7.53%	6.86%
Have ever used other drugs	9.17%	10.34%

*Note: For the purposes of this study, the researchers defined problematic gaming as unsuccessful attempts to cut back on gaming, irresistible urges to play, and experiencing growing tension that can only be relieved by gaming.

Scale goes up to 18 percent.

Source: Rani A. Desai et al., "Video-Gaming Among High School Students: Health Correlates, Gender Differences, and Problematic Gaming," *Pediatrics*, December 2010. http://pediatrics.aapublications.org.

- A study published in the December 2010 issue of the medical journal *Pediatrics*, which involved 4,028 teenagers, revealed that of those who played video games, about **5 percent** showed addictive tendencies.

Problem Gamblers Favor Live Poker Games

Whether the ability to gamble on the Internet contributes to gambling addiction is a controversial issue. According to the 2010 British Gambling Prevalence Survey, which involved nearly 8,000 adult gamblers, online gambling was not as common among problem gamblers as poker at a club or pub or betting on dog races but was more prevalent than other types of gambling.

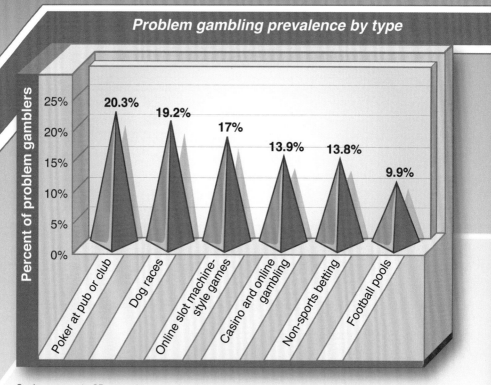

Problem gambling prevalence by type

Scale goes up to 25 percent.

Source: Heather Wardle et al., British Gambling Prevalence Survey 2010, February 2011. www.gambling.commission.gov.

- According to a 2009 report by Canadian researchers Robert Wood and Robert Williams, online gamblers in Canada spend an average of **$541 per month** on gambling, compared with offline gamblers, who spend an average of **$67 per month**.

- A study published in April 2011 by Harvard University psychologist Howard Shaffer found that despite the rapid growth of online gambling, the rate of pathological gambling has remained **relatively stable** over the past 35 years.

- A study published in 2009 by a team of researchers from Taiwan found that regions of the brain associated with **substance abuse** cravings also appear to be activated in gaming addicts when they view images of video games.

- A study published in 2010 by a team of German researchers found that **1.5 percent to 3.5 percent** of teenage Internet users in Germany show signs of gaming addiction.

- A 2011 study by Canadian psychologist Jeffrey Derevensky found that **8 percent** of participating adolescents between the ages of 14 and 17 were at risk for developing gambling disorders, and almost **5 percent** were already gambling addicts.

- A February 2011 study involving over 3,000 children in Singapore found that between **7.6 percent and 9.9 percent** were addicted to gaming.

Can People Recover from Online Addiction?

66While there is no consensus regarding the clinical status of Internet addiction, there appears to be significant demand for treatment for Internet-related problems.99

—Mark D. Griffiths, a psychologist and gambling addiction expert from the United Kingdom.

66Unfortunately, evidence-based treatment for problematic Internet use is not well established and existing sources of help are not yet widely available, a fact that is not likely to change while funding for mental health services is on the chopping block.99

—Michael Friedman, an adjunct associate professor at the Columbia University Schools of Social Work and Public Health.

When David Tang, a 14-year-old boy from China, slapped his father for unplugging the computer, his parents were stunned as well as angry. The teen had been playing an online game for over 20 hours and had repeatedly ignored requests to sign off and get some rest. "I was so shocked," says the elder Tang. "My son is a nice kid with proper manners. I don't understand how he suddenly became like this. At that second, his immediate reaction was to beat me."[63] Tang's parents have grown increasingly worried that their son is addicted to the Internet. They believe that he needs help but are frightened by stories of youths in their country who were beaten, given electroshock therapy, and subjected to other cruel and inhumane practices. In lieu of treatment, the Tangs decided to try spending more time with their son. If he does not show signs of improvement, they will make a decision about how best to help him recover.

A Tough Addiction to Beat

Overcoming online addiction can be difficult. The difficulty can be attributed to several factors, one of which is denial: Like other addicts, Internet addicts often have a hard time acknowledging that they have a serious problem and need help. Or, they may find it unbearable to even think about giving up their favorite online activities. Another hurdle is that unlike drug or alcohol addiction, from which abusers can recover if they stop ingesting substances, giving up the Internet is virtually impossible since it is an integral part of daily life. But according to Kimberly S. Young, complete abstinence is not necessary. "You don't have to go 'cold turkey' in order to deal with this disorder," says Young. "Since the Internet is a productive tool when used properly, it [is] important to find a balance between Internet use and other life activities."[64]

> **Unlike drug or alcohol addiction, from which abusers can recover if they stop ingesting substances, giving up the Internet is virtually impossible since it is an integral part of daily life.**

Jerald J. Block, a psychiatrist who specializes in compulsive computer use, says that not only is cutting off Internet access too quickly unnecessary, doing so can be dangerous. For many online addicts, the computer has been their primary source of relationship building, as well as a conduit for dealing with difficult emotions. For that to be suddenly taken away is traumatic, says Block, and can lead to aggressive behavior, violence toward others, and possibly suicide.

Yet for Ryan G. Van Cleave, who was severely addicted to online gaming, abruptly cutting himself off was the only way to stop the destruction of his life. By the time he admitted how bad his problem was, he had been addicted to *World of Warcraft* for three years and was playing 60 hours a week. One winter night in 2007, Van Cleave was filled with despair over what he had done to himself and his family. He went to the Arlington Memorial Bridge, stood at the edge, and gave serious thought to jumping into the frigid water below. Then in a moment of clarity, he stopped himself because he realized that he did not want to die.

> **People who suffer from online addiction often have trouble finding professionals who can help them.**

What Van Cleave *did* want was to get his life back and mend his relationship with his wife and children. He believed there was still a chance for that to happen—but only if he gave up gaming for good. He walked away from the bridge and went home, deleted *World of Warcraft* from his computer, and did not reinstall it. That was the beginning of a new, addiction-free life for Van Cleave, and he never again returned to gaming.

One Step at a Time

People who suffer from online addiction often have trouble finding professionals who can help them. Although treatment programs for drug and alcohol addiction are plentiful, the same is not true of online addiction. This was a source of frustration for a woman named Pauline, who had been addicted to the Internet for years before seeking help. She saw a therapist for a while and benefited from the sessions, but still could not overcome her addiction. So, she talked to a friend who belonged to Alcoholics Anonymous (AA) and told Pauline about the 12-step program. Armed with that information she started her own group, which she called Internet Addicts Anonymous.

Pauline developed program guidelines modeled after those of AA. She created a website where she wrote about her personal struggle with Internet addiction and also held a series of meetings at a local community center. There was little interest in the program, however, and few people attended meetings, so Pauline dissolved the group. Yet even though the program itself was short-lived, the process of putting it together had helped her chart a path for her own recovery. Since that time she has made a great deal of progress, although she doubts that she has fully recovered from online addiction. "I'm self-aware enough not to say that I'm cured," she says, "but it doesn't feel unmanageable."[65]

Therapy Helps Healing

Many patients who seek treatment for online addiction have made significant progress through therapy. Addicted children and adolescents, for instance, often benefit from family-based therapy, which opens lines of communication and helps parents learn to set appropriate limits. Another type, known as cognitive behavioral therapy (CBT), has also proved to be effective in treating online addiction. CBT focuses on identifying unhealthy, negative, or irrational beliefs that might lead to addiction behavior such as using the Internet as an escape from real life.

Therapy played a major role in Kevin Roberts's recovery from online gaming addiction. He did a great deal of soul searching during his sessions with a therapist and learned many things about himself that he had not been able to face before. One revelation was that he had turned to the online world as a remedy for his inability to form real-life relationships. Says Roberts:

> I developed an addiction that kept me isolated from people. As I look back to high school and college, I see that I had not developed the ability to read social cues. I neither understood how to maintain friendships, nor did I have a clue about how to help them grow. When I finally did start the process of recovery from my cyber addiction, it was a long while before I could navigate through friendships and relationships successfully.[66]

Also through therapy, Roberts learned to accept responsibility for his own actions, rather than place blame elsewhere. "Instead of accepting that my choices created my life," he says, "I blamed other people and situations that were beyond my control." This, says Roberts, was the key to his recovery from gaming addiction. Even when cravings seemed overwhelming, "I realized I had the power to make a choice."[67]

A New Start

By the time a young man named Nick reached out for help, he had become hopelessly attached to the Internet. He had not been happy for a long time, and originally turned to online activities in an attempt to escape from the realities of life: "It provided an easy way of forgetting my troubles," says Nick, "and a safer means of social contact, so I could tell myself that things weren't really that bad. Of course, it didn't help with actually solving my problems." As aware as he was of being in trouble, Nick was not convinced that he was addicted. "I was still eating well," he says, "maintaining good hygiene, and keeping tidy: the opposite of the conventional view of the Internet addict, right? I felt perfectly capable of taking care of myself."[68] Finally, Nick could no longer deny that he was an addict, and he turned to an Internet addiction program called reSTART for help.

Located in Fall City, Washington, reSTART is a 45-day program that admits no more than six patients per session. Based on personalized assessments, treatment regimens are developed on a customized basis and include individual and group counseling with professionally trained staff, life skills and vocational coaching, 12-step meetings, and spiritual recovery sessions. The reSTART program also involves a wide variety of recreational activities such as nature hikes, high adventure outings, health and fitness programs such as yoga and jogging, and nutritional education, as well as volunteer work for community service projects.

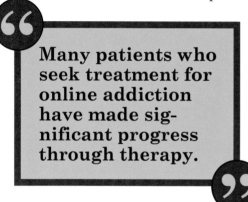

Many patients who seek treatment for online addiction have made significant progress through therapy.

Nick gained a great deal from his stay at reSTART. He learned that his stress and depression were symptoms of deeper problems such as anxiety and fear, and that immersing himself in the Internet was keeping him from dealing with those problems. He also found that being part of a group was invaluable, as he explains: "As we learned together, we gained knowledge of ourselves, others, how we relate to each other, and how we relate to objects—things like the Internet. Everyone involved in the program was more than just a participant, counselor or teacher; we became true friends." When his treatment was complete, Nick was hopeful about the future—but admittedly a little scared, too. "As I leave reSTART and begin to change my life," he says, "I am faced with intimidating challenges. Many of them are ones which I could not deal with before. However, I now have the serenity and mindfulness to cope with difficult times and the social connections to make my life fulfilling."[69]

Boot Camp Horrors

Unlike in the United States, where online addiction treatment centers are scarce, several Asian countries have opened hundreds of these facilities—and the methods used in some have been extreme, abusive, and even deadly. One such facility is the Qihang Salvation Training Camp in rural China. Although Chinese officials touted it as a recovery center that focused on therapy and healing, a far different story has been told by children and adults who have actually seen what goes on. A January 2010 *Wired* article explains: "Its treatment regimen revolved around intense martial drills, which began at sunrise with a harsh whistle and sometimes didn't end until after midnight. Campers who couldn't complete the required laps or push-ups were beaten. Screams could be heard constantly."[70]

When Deng Fei decided to send his 15-year-old son to the Qihang boot camp, he knew nothing of its sordid reputation. After seeing a television advertisement for the facility, which showed a family standing together and smiling, he thought it looked like a legitimate, safe place. His son, Deng Senshan, had become so addicted to online gaming that he desperately needed help, so his family dropped him off at the facility in August 2009.

Like all newcomers to the Qihang Salvation Training Camp, Deng Senshan began his stay in a "confinement room," where he was ordered to face the wall. When he refused, counselors began hitting him. Later that evening he and three other teens were instructed to run laps around the basketball courts, and Deng Senshan stumbled and fell. He was dragged

> **Unlike in the United States, where online addiction treatment centers are scarce, several Asian countries have opened hundreds of these facilities—and the methods used in some have been extreme, abusive, and even deadly.**

away by a counselor and struck so hard with a wooden chair leg that it broke, and when he tried to escape, he was beaten with a plastic stool. A security guard, who watched from the edge of the school grounds, was shocked at how brutally Deng Senshan was being treated, and he said to his wife: "This boy will be lucky if he lives through the night."[71] Deng Senshan was not "lucky," however. Before dawn, just 14 hours after he had arrived at Qihang camp, the boy was dead.

At least a dozen people were arrested and jailed for Deng Senshan's death, and the local government was sharply criticized for its role in Qihang's brutal tactics. In November 2010 China's Ministry of Health drafted new guidelines for boot camps, with physical punishment and other cruel practices banned. Some believe this is a hopeful sign that things will continue to improve, while others are inclined to believe that it is nothing more than damage control on the part of the Chinese government.

Hope for the Future

People who suffer from online addiction can and do recover, but it is a challenging disorder to treat. Many addicts do not want help out of fear that giving up their Internet "lifeline" would be too much to bear, while others deny that they have a problem at all. Even when addicts do want to be treated, facilities that specialize in online addiction are scarce in the United States—and in some Asian countries "therapy" is nothing short of inhumane. In the future, as online addiction becomes better understood, treatment options will undoubtedly increase, and those who suffer will have a better chance at recovery.

Can People Recover
from Online Addiction?

66 **Growing research suggests that some individuals with internet addiction are at significant risk and merit our professional care and treatment.** 99

—Ronald Pies, "Should DSM-V Designate 'Internet Addiction' a Mental Disorder?," *Psychiatry*, February 2009. www.ncbi.nlm.nih.gov.

Pies is a psychiatry professor at State University of New York Upstate Medical University and a clinical professor of psychiatry at Tufts University School of Medicine in Boston.

66 **Hospitals and clinics have emerged with outpatient treatment services for Internet addiction, addiction rehabilitation centers have admitted new cases of Internet addicts, and college campuses have started support groups to help students who are addicted.** 99

—Kimberly S. Young and Cristiano Nabuco de Abreu, eds., *Internet Addiction: A Handbook and Guide to Evaluation and Treatment*. Hoboken, NJ: Wiley, 2011.

Young is the director of the Center for Internet Addiction, and Abreu is a psychologist at the University of São Paulo in Brazil.

* Editor's Note: While the definition of a primary source can be narrowly or broadly defined, for the purposes of Compact Research, a primary source consists of: 1) results of original research presented by an organization or researcher; 2) eyewitness accounts of events, personal experience, or work experience; 3) first-person editorials offering pundits' opinions; 4) government officials presenting political plans and/or policies; 5) representatives of organizations presenting testimony or policy.

Primary Source Quotes

" Research has shown that as with many behavioral addictions, cognitive behavioral therapy provides the most effective way to treat Internet addictions, as do self-help and twelve-step groups. "

—Howard Padwa and Jacob Cunningham, eds., *Addiction: A Reference Encyclopedia*. Santa Barbara, CA: Greenwood, 2010.

Padwa is a public policy researcher, and Cunningham teaches history at Hebrew Union College in Los Angeles.

" Be proactive, get educated on technology (you can do it) and get involved. The best way to protect your family from the dark side of the Internet is to stand between them and the Internet. "

—Steve Ensley, "Study: Internet Addiction a Growing Problem Among Youth," Steve Ensley, February 2, 2012. http://steveensley.com.

Ensley is an Internet safety specialist from Florida.

" When I finally did start the process of recovery from my cyber addiction, it was a long while before I could navigate through friendships and relationships successfully. "

—Kevin Roberts, "Confessions of a Cyber Junkie," *USA Today*, March 2011.

Roberts, who recovered from online addiction, conducts support groups for teens and adults who struggle with the same addiction.

" To the extent that the Internet-related problem may stem from another diagnosis (e.g., a patient with severe social anxiety who starts leading a 'virtual' life at the expense of offline interactions), it might improve as the primary condition is addressed. "

—Elias Aboujaoude, "Problematic Internet Use: An Overview," *World Psychiatry*, June 2010. www.ncbi.nlm.nih.gov.

Aboujaoude is a psychiatrist and the director of Stanford University's Impulse Control Disorders Clinic.

66 It's not the technology (whether it be the Internet, a book, the telephone, or the television) that is important or addicting—it's the behavior. And behaviors are easily treatable by traditional cognitive-behavior techniques in psychotherapy. 99

—John M. Grohol, "Internet Addiction Guide," Psych Central, January 5, 2012. http://psychcentral.com.

Grohol is a psychologist and the publisher of the Psych Central website.

66 If your various types of 'screen time' are taking over your life, it's time to take stock. Wanting to change is the necessary first step. 99

—Anthony Komaroff, "Is Too Much 'Screen Time' Unhealthy?," Ask Doctor K., December 16, 2011. www.askdoctork.com.

Komaroff is a doctor of internal medicine and professor of medicine at Harvard Medical School.

Facts and Illustrations

Can People Recover from Online Addiction?

- South Korea's Minister of Public Administration and Safety reports that the number of the country's teenage Internet addicts declined from over **1 million** in 2007 to **938,000** in 2009, which is largely due to government counseling programs.

- According to psychiatrists Timothy Liu and Marc N. Potenza, the only type of Internet addiction treatment that has been examined in evidence-based studies is **cognitive behavioral therapy**, and results have been promising.

- A 2010 paper by online addiction expert Elias Aboujaoude cites a study that involved 114 adult Internet addicts treated with cognitive behavioral therapy; the study found that most participants were able to **control their symptoms** by the eighth session and improvement was sustained over a six-month period.

- At the conclusion of a 2011 study that found **4 percent** of college students were affected by online addiction, researcher Dimitri A. Christakis and his colleagues recommended that colleges implement awareness campaigns both for prevention and to help identify students who suffer from problematic Internet use and may need treatment.

- Oregon psychiatrist Jerald J. Block states that cutting off an online addict's Internet access too suddenly can lead to **aggressive behavior**, including **violence** against others and/or **suicide attempts**.

Program Helps Online Addicts Recover

The first inpatient recovery program for Internet addicts opened in Fall City, Washington, in 2009. To determine the effectiveness of the program, which is called reSTART, the group conducted a study of 21 participants and found that 74 percent showed significant improvement.

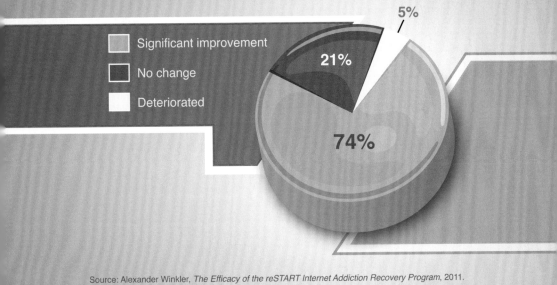

Legend:
- Significant improvement
- No change
- Deteriorated

5%
21%
74%

Source: Alexander Winkler, *The Efficacy of the reSTART Internet Addiction Recovery Program*, 2011. www.netaddictionrecovery.com.

- According to the addiction treatment group Elements Behavioral Health, unlike addictions to alcohol and drugs, **total abstinence** is not usually an effective treatment for Internet addiction; rather, learning to use the Internet in **moderation** should be the goal.

- According to psychiatrists Timothy Liu and Marc N. Potenza, multiple **treatment centers** and groups who specialize in Internet addiction are emerging in both online and offline settings.

- A report published in September 2010 by researchers from the United States and Israel states that both behavioral and substance addictions respond to treatment that combines some form of **psychotherapy and medications**.

How Therapy Helps Online Addicts

Many people who suffer from online addiction can benefit from professional counseling. Common strategies used by therapists in sessions with teen addicts include identifying triggers and training in interpersonal skills.

Identifying triggers involved in Internet addiction	These include the thoughts and feelings that precede the teen's use of the Internet.
Changing the environment in which the teen normally interacts with the computer	This may involve altering the associations the teen has with the Internet, or decreasing the reinforcement he or she receives from nonstop Internet use.
Training in interpersonal communication and social skills development	Many teens who have become addicted to the Internet are socially withdrawn and lack the ability to communicate easily with others on a face-to-face basis.
Awareness of the risk of relapse	Effective treatment will concentrate on relapse prevention skills, including identifying situations that may trigger the teen's falling back into excessive use of the Internet and putting together an action plan for dealing with such situations if they occur.
Referral to support group (may be modeled after Alcoholics Anonymous or other "12-step" groups)	Interacting with others who suffer from online addiction may be beneficial for addicted teens.

Source: Suzanne Kane, "Teens and Internet Addiction," *Addiction Treatment Magazine*, January 19, 2010. www.addictiontreatmentmagazine.com.

- To help fight the growing problem of Internet addiction in their countries, South Korea has opened an estimated **200 treatment centers**, and China more than **300**.

- According to a 2010 paper by psychiatrist and online addiction expert Elias Aboujaoude, family therapy that improves communication and teaches **family monitoring** of Internet use can be beneficial for children and adolescents who suffer from online addiction.

- Because online addiction often coexists with mental disorders such as **depression** and **attention-deficit/hyperactivity disorder**, Taiwan researcher Chih-Hung Ko and colleagues recommend that physicians screen for these disorders before recommending treatment.

- According to British gambling addiction specialist Ian Semel, women who have become addicted to Internet gambling are much more likely to seek treatment from **online resources** than by calling or visiting a therapist in person.

Key People and Advocacy Groups

Elias Aboujaoude: A psychiatrist and Internet addiction expert who directs the Impulse Control Disorders Clinic at Stanford University School of Medicine.

American Psychiatric Association (APA): The world's largest and most prestigious psychiatric organization and the publisher of the DSM.

Jerald J. Block: A psychiatrist at Oregon Health and Science University and an advocate for Internet addiction to be included in the DSM.

Hilarie Cash: A psychiatrist who cofounded reSTART, the first inpatient online addiction recovery program in the United States.

Center for Internet Addiction: A group founded by psychologist Kimberly S. Young in 1995 to help people who are addicted to the Internet.

Ivan Goldberg: A psychiatrist who coined the phrase "Internet addiction disorder" in 1995 as a spoof on the tendency of the APA to label all excessive behaviors as mental disorders or addictions.

David Greenfield: A psychologist and noted computer addiction expert who founded the Center for Internet and Technology Addiction in West Hartford, Connecticut.

Mark D. Griffiths: A psychologist and gambling addiction expert from the United Kingdom who was one of the first mental health professionals to research online addiction.

Maressa Hecht Orzack: A psychologist, Internet addiction expert, and founder of Computer Addiction Services at McLean Hospital, one of the first psychiatric facilities in the United States to treat online addiction.

Cosette Dawna Rae: An online addiction specialist who cofounded reSTART, the first inpatient online addiction recovery program in the United States.

Kimberly S. Young: A psychologist and Internet addiction expert who was the first to extensively research and write about how excessive Internet use affected people.

Chronology

1935
In their book *The Psychology of Radio*, psychologist Gordon Allport and researcher Hadley Cantril express their concern about the potential psychological effects of habitual radio listening.

1998
Planet Poker becomes the first website to offer multiplayer online poker games.

1995
New York psychiatrist Ivan Goldberg proposes the phrase "Internet addiction disorder" as a spoof on the American Psychiatric Association's tendency to label all excessive behaviors as mental disorders.

1985
Steve Case and Jim Kimsey found Quantum Computer Services, which later becomes America Online, a service that is especially popular for its chat rooms.

1935   **1985**   **1995**

1989
As part of her doctoral dissertation, Margaret A. Shotton publishes the book *Computer Addiction? A Study of Computer Dependency*, in which she investigates cases of obsessive computer use among people in the United Kingdom.

1994
Psychologist Kimberly S. Young posts a questionnaire in an online forum to evaluate whether people feel addicted to the Internet, and she receives responses from all over the United States and several other countries.

1991
Swiss computer expert Tim Berners-Lee announces his creation of software and a point-and-click browser, thus launching the World Wide Web.

1996
Psychologist Kimberly S. Young is the first to publish a detailed case report of problematic Internet use, titled "Psychology of Computer Use: XL. Addictive Use of the Internet: A Case That Breaks the Stereotype."

1997
The first social networking website, SixDegrees, is launched, based on the idea that everyone is linked to everybody else via six degrees of separation.

2012
Researchers from Greece release a study showing that teens who are pathological Internet users are more likely to abuse drugs and alcohol; the study also links substance abuse and excessive Internet use with personality traits such as aggressiveness, recklessness, and impulsiveness.

1999
Psychologist David Greenfield founds the Center for Internet and Technology Addiction in West Hartford, Connecticut.

2005
The video-sharing website YouTube goes online and allows users to upload, share, and view videos.

2010
The APA issues a news release stating that the DSM-V will include a category for behavioral (non-substance) addictions, but Internet addiction will not be included due to insufficient research data.

2000

2010

2004
The social networking site Facebook is launched as a closed virtual community for students at Harvard University. After the site is opened to the public, it soon soars in popularity among users throughout the world.

2009
reSTART, the first inpatient treatment facility in the United States that is exclusively devoted to Internet addiction, opens in Fall City, Washington.

2007
The American Medical Association issues an announcement in which it supports the inclusion of Internet/video game addiction in the next revision of the DSM; within days the group reverses its position, saying that more research is needed.

2011
The American Society of Addiction Medicine recognizes addiction as a brain disease that is reflected in someone's pathological pursuit of reward and/or relief by the use of substances or behaviors such as compulsive Internet use.

Related Organizations

American Gaming Association (AGA)

1299 Pennsylvania Ave. NW, Suite 1175
Washington, DC 20004
phone: (202) 552-2675 • fax: (202) 552-2676
e-mail: info@americangaming.org • website: www.americangaming.org

The AGA's goal is to help create a better understanding of the online gaming industry by providing information to the public, elected officials, other decision makers, and the media. Its website's search engine produces a number of informative articles about online gaming and gambling.

American Psychiatric Association (APA)

1000 Wilson Blvd., Suite 1825
Arlington, VA 22209
phone: (703) 907-7300; toll-free: (888) 357-7924
e-mail: apa@psych.org • website: www.psych.org

With 36,000 psychiatric physician members, the APA is the world's largest psychiatric organization. Its website provides information about the DSM, as well as the *Psychiatric News* online magazine, research reports, and a search engine that produces a number of articles.

Center for Internet Addiction

PO Box 72
Bradford, PA 16701
phone: (814) 451-2405 • fax: (814) 368-9560
website: www.netaddiction.com

The Center for Internet Addiction offers counseling for individuals, couples, and families for problematic Internet use and related issues. Its website offers numerous articles; frequently asked questions; information sheets on issues such as compulsive web surfing, online gambling, and cybersex/cyberporn; statistics; and a link to the *Recovery* blog.

Center for Internet and Technology Addiction

17 S. Highland St.
West Hartford, CT 06119
phone: (860) 561-8727 • fax: (860) 561-8424
e-mail: drdave@virtual-addiction.com
website: www.virtual-addiction.com

The Center for Internet and Technology Addiction provides therapeutic services, information, and resources about online addiction, social media, and problems with all forms of digital technology. A wealth of information is available through its website, including articles, news releases, lectures by online addiction expert David Greenfield, and videos.

Illinois Institute for Addiction Recovery

5409 N. Knoxville Ave.
Peoria, IL 61614
phone: (309) 691-1055; toll-free: (800) 522-3784
website: www.addictionrecov.org

The Illinois Institute for Addiction Recovery provides treatment for all types of chemical and behavioral addictions. Its website features separate sections for Internet and gaming addictions and offers information about warning signs, effects, and recovery. The site also offers news releases and video clips, as well as current and archived issues of the *Paradigm* online magazine.

Network for Internet Investigation and Research Australia (NIIRA)

website: www.niira.org.au

The NIIRA is an online resource that was developed by leaders and specialists in the field of Internet-related disorders. The site offers a number of informative articles about online addiction and addresses such topics as proposed diagnostic criteria, why the Internet is so attractive to young people, and "On Virtual Addiction."

Online Gamers Anonymous

PO Box 67
Osceola, WI 54020
phone: (612) 245-1115
e-mail: olga@olganon.org • website: www.olganon.org

Online Gamers Anonymous is a fellowship group that exists to help people recover from excessive game playing. Its website offers separate message boards for gamers and families of gamers, information about meetings (including those on Skype), and links to news articles about gaming addiction.

On-Line Therapy Institute

PO Box 392
Highlands, NJ 07732
phone: (877) 773-5591
e-mail: info@onlinetherapyinstitute.com
website: www.onlinetherapyinstitute.com

The On-Line Therapy Institute disseminates information about research, education, and training, on topics such as Internet addiction, online gaming, social networking, and "virtual worlds." Although primarily designed for professionals, the site offers some informative publications about online addiction, such as *TILT* magazine.

reSTART Internet and Technology Addiction Recovery

1001 290th Ave. SE
Fall City, WA 98024-7403
phone: (800) 682-6934 • fax: (888) 788-3419
e-mail: contactus@netaddictionrecovery.com
website: www.netaddictionrecovery.com

reSTART is a treatment facility whose mission is to help launch tech-dependent youths and adults back into the real world. Its website features news articles, personal stories, information about treatment programs, and a comprehensive technology section with answers to many questions about online addiction and related problems.

For Further Research

Books

Elias Aboujaoude, *Virtually You: The Dangerous Powers of the E-personality*. New York: Norton, 2011.

Holly Cefrey, *Frequently Asked Questions About Online Gaming Addiction*. New York: Rosen, 2010.

Samuel C. McQuade, Sarah E. Gentry, and James P. Colt, *Internet Addiction and Online Gaming*. New York: Chelsea House, 2011.

Hannah O. Price, ed., *Internet Addiction*. Hauppauge, NY: Nova Science, 2011.

Kevin Roberts, *Cyber Junkie: Escape the Game and Internet Trap*. Center City, MN: Hazelden, 2010.

Ryan G. Van Cleave, *Unplugged: My Journey into the Dark World of Internet Game Addiction*. Deerfield Beach, FL: Health Communications, 2010.

Kimberly S. Young and Cristiano Nabuco de Abreu, eds., *Internet Addiction: A Handbook and Guide to Evaluation and Treatment*. Hoboken, NJ: Wiley, 2011.

Periodicals

Greg Beato, "Internet Addiction: What Once Was Parody May Soon Be Diagnosis," *Reason*, August/September 2010.

Economist, "Addicted? Really?," March 12, 2011.

Katie Hafner, "'Defriending' Facebook," *New York Times Upfront*, March 15, 2010.

Tara Parker-Pope, "An Ugly Toll of Technology: Impatience and Forgetfulness," *New York Times*, June 6, 2010.

Matt Richtel, "U.S. Cracks Down on Online Gambling," *New York Times*, April 15, 2011.

Kevin Roberts, "Confessions of a Cyber Junkie," *USA Today*, March 2011.

Rebecca Rosen, "Can You Get Treatment for Your Internet Addiction?," *Atlantic*, August 26, 2011.

Christopher S. Stewart, "The Lost Boy," *Wired*, February 2010.

Carolyn Sun, "Online Cravings," *Newsweek International*, October 24, 2011.

Kayla Webley, "It's Time to Confront Your Facebook Addiction," *Time*, July 8, 2010.

William Weir, "Is Gambling More Addictive Online?," *Hartford (CT) Courant*, December 30, 2011.

Internet Sources

Josh Axelrad, "Online Gambling May Be Too Powerful for Regulation," *Guardian* (Manchester), April 21, 2011. www.guardian.co.uk/commentisfree/2011/apr/21/online-gambling-regulations.

Seth Borenstein, "No Wikipedia? What If the Internet Went Down?," Yahoo News, January 18, 2012. http://news.yahoo.com/no-wikipedia-internet-went-down-233050046.html.

Suzanne Choney, "Students Worldwide Share Mobile Addiction," *Digital Life* (blog), *Today.com*, April 7, 2011. http://digitallife.today.msnbc.msn.com/_news/2011/04/07/6425175-students-worldwide-share-mobile-addiction.

Tamara Cohen, "Teenage Video Game Players Have Brains 'Like Gambling Addicts,'" *Mail Online*, November 2011. www.dailymail.co.uk/sciencetech/article-2061983/Teenage-video-game-players-brains-like-gambling-addicts.html.

Elements Behavioral Health, "Teens and Internet Addiction," *Addiction Treatment Magazine*, January 19, 2010. www.addictiontreatmentmagazine.com/addiction/internet-addiction/teens-and-internet-addiction.

Ed Grabianowski, "How Computer Addiction Works," HowStuffWorks. http://computer.howstuffworks.com/internet/basics/computer-addiction3.htm.

John M. Grohol, "Internet Addiction Guide," Psych Central, January 5, 2012. http://psychcentral.com/netaddiction.

Wednesday Martin, "Teens and the Internet: How Much Is Too Much?,"

Psychology Today, April 6, 2010. www.psychologytoday.com/blog/
stepmonster/201004/teens-and-the-internet-how-much-is-too-much.

Genevra Pittman, "How Many Teens Have 'Internet Addiction'?,"
Reuters, May 19, 2011. www.reuters.com/article/2011/05/19/us-teens
-internet-addiction-idUSTRE74I6OA20110519.

Kimberly S. Young, "Internet Addiction over the Decade: A Personal
Look Back," *World Psychiatry*, June 2010. www.ncbi.nlm.nih.gov/
pmc/articles/PMC2911082/pdf/wpa020091.pdf.

Source Notes

Overview

1. Winston Ross, "A World Wide Woe," *Daily Beast*, October 7, 2009. www.thedailybeast.com.
2. Ross, "A World Wide Woe."
3. Mark D. Griffiths, "Why Anything Can Be Addictive," BBC, November 24, 2011. www.bbc.co.uk.
4. Philip Tam, "Dr. Philip Tam on 'Internet Addiction' or Problematic Internet Use," *Practice What I Preach: A Child Psychiatrist on Parenting* (blog), November 1, 2010. http://psychiatristparent.wordpress.com.
5. American Psychiatric Association, "*DSM-5* Proposed Revisions Include New Category of Addiction and Related Disorders: *New Category of Behavioral Addictions Also Proposed*," February 10, 2010. www.dsm5.org.
6. Quoted in Elias Aboujaoude and Lorrin M. Koran, eds., *Impulse Control Disorders*. New York: Cambridge University Press, 2010, p. 171.
7. Elias Aboujaoude, *Virtually You: The Dangerous Powers of the E-personality*. New York: Norton, 2011, p. 317.
8. Dimitri A. Christakis et al., "Problematic Internet Usage in US College Students: A Pilot Study," *BMC Medicine*, 2011. www.biomedcentral.com.
9. Kimberly S. Young, "eBay Addiction," Center for Internet Addiction, February 25, 2011. www.netaddiction.com.
10. Kimberly S. Young, "What Are the Risk Factors Involved with Internet Addiction?," HealthyPlace, January 12, 2012. www.healthyplace.com.
11. Kevin Roberts, "Confessions of a Cyber Junkie," book excerpt, *USA Today*, March 2011, p. 60.
12. Roberts, "Confessions of a Cyber Junkie," p. 60.
13. Elements Behavioral Health, "Teens and Internet Addiction," *Addiction Treatment Magazine*, January 19, 2010. www.addictiontreatmentmagazine.com.
14. Aboujaoude, *Virtually You*, p. 223.
15. Michael Fenichel, "Facebook Addiction Disorder (FAD)," January 14, 2012. www.fenichel.com.
16. Erin Clark, "I Check My E-mail 100 Times a Day," *Marie Claire*, March 2009, p. 220.
17. Quoted in Dave Mosher, "High Wired: Does Addictive Internet Use Restructure the Brain?," *Scientific American*, June 17, 2011. www.scientificamerican.com.
18. Roberts, "Confessions of a Cyber Junkie," p. 60.
19. Kimberly S. Young, "Online Gambling," Center for Internet Addiction, February 25, 2011. www.netaddiction.com.
20. Quoted in Aboujaoude and Koran, *Impulse Control Disorders*, p. 167.
21. Quoted in Mosher, "High Wired."
22. Kimberly S. Young, "How Do You Treat Internet Addiction?," HealthyPlace, January 12, 2012. www.healthyplace.com.

Is Online Addiction Real?

23. Quoted in E. Guy Coffee, "Internet-Addiction-Support-Group for Those with Acute or Chronic Internet Addiction Disorder," Heidelberg University, March 16, 1995. http://web.urz.uni-heidelberg.de.
24. David Wallis, "Just Click No," *New Yorker*, January 13, 1997. www.psycom.net.

25. Kimberly S. Young, "Psychology of Computer Use: XL. Addictive Use of the Internet: A Case That Breaks the Stereotype," *Psychological Reports*, 1996. www.netaddiction.com.

26. Kimberly S. Young, *Caught in the Net*. New York: John Wiley & Sons, 1998, p. 11.

27. Kimberly S. Young, "Internet Addiction over the Decade: A Personal Look Back," *World Psychiatry*, June 2010. www.ncbi.nlm.nih.gov.

28. Quoted in Harry G. Levine, "The Discovery of Addiction: Changing Conceptions of Habitual Drunkenness in America," *Journal of Studies on Alcohol*, 1978. http://dragon.soc.qc.cuny.edu.

29. American Society of Addiction Medicine, "Internet Addiction Could Be Warning Sign of Substance Use in Teens," news release, February 13, 2012. www.asam.org.

30. Quoted in Brenda Patoine, "Is 'Internet Addiction' a Psychiatric Disorder?," Dana Foundation, July 6, 2009. www.dana.org.

31. Todd Essig, "DSM-5 Opens the Diagnostic Door to 'Internet Addiction,'" *True/Slant*, February 10, 2010. http://trueslant.com.

32. Quoted in Nicholas K. Geranios, "When Computers Become Addictive," *Chicago Tribune*, October 6, 2009. www.chicagotribune.com.

33. Quoted in Polly Curtis, "Can You Really Be Addicted to the Internet?," *Guardian* (Manchester), January 12, 2012. www.guardian.co.uk.

34. Quoted in Randy Dotinga, "Could Internet Addiction Disrupt Brain's Connections?," *U.S. News & World Report*, January 12, 2012. http://health.usnews.com.

35. Young, "Internet Addiction over the Decade."

Can People Get Addicted to Social Networking?

36. April H., "Teens on Facebook: When Does It Become Too Much?," *Huffington Post*, November 11, 2011. www.huffingtonpost.com.

37. April H., "Teens on Facebook."

38. Daria J. Kuss and Mark D. Griffiths, "Online Social Networking and Addiction—a Review of the Psychological Literature," *International Journal of Environmental Research and Public Health*, August 29, 2011. www.mdpi.com.

39. Kuss and Griffiths, "Online Social Networking and Addiction—a Review of the Psychological Literature."

40. Kuss and Griffiths, "Online Social Networking and Addiction—a Review of the Psychological Literature."

41. Elements Behavioral Health, "Watch Out for Addiction to Social Networking Sites," *Addiction Treatment Magazine*, June 16, 2010. www.addictiontreatmentmagazine.com.

42. Elements Behavioral Health, "Watch Out for Addiction to Social Networking Sites."

43. Quoted in Sharon Gaudin, "Social Networking Addicts Updating from Bed, Bathroom," *Computerworld*, March 17, 2010. www.computerworld.com.

44. Laurel Snyder, "Addicted to Twitter," *Salon*, August 15, 2009. www.salon.com.

45. Snyder, "Addicted to Twitter."

46. Snyder, "Addicted to Twitter."

47. Snyder, "Addicted to Twitter."

48. Snyder, "Addicted to Twitter."

How Serious a Problem Is Compulsive Online Gaming and Gambling?

49. Douglas A. Gentile et al., "Pathological Video Game Use Among Youths: A

Two-Year Longitudinal Study," *Pediatrics*, January 17, 2011. http://pediatrics.aappublications.org.

50. Gentile et al., "Pathological Video Game Use Among Youths."

51. Kimberly S. Young, "Online Gaming," Center for Internet Addiction, November 14, 2011. www.netaddiction.com.

52. Quoted in Nicholas K. Geranios, "Addicted to the Internet? There's Rehab for That," MSNBC, September 3, 2009. http://rss.msnbc.msn.com.

53. Quoted in Holly Hines, "Former Student Addicted to World of Warcraft," *Daily Iowan* (Iowa City, IA), October 28, 2009. www.dailyiowan.com.

54. Quoted in Justin McCurry, "South Koreans Face the Social Impact of Virtual Obsession," *Taipei Times*, July 19, 2010. www.taipeitimes.com.

55. Leon, "PC Bang," ESLSouthKorea, 2011. www.eslsouthkorea.net.

56. Leon, "PC Bang."

57. Quoted in William Weir, "Is Gambling More Addictive Online?," *Hartford (CT) Courant*, December 30, 2011. http://articles.courant.com.

58. Josh Axelrad, "Online Gambling May Be Too Powerful for Regulation," *Guardian* (Manchester), April 21, 2011. www.guardian.co.uk.

59. Josh Axelrad, "Losing My Book Advance Taught Me to Write," *Huffington Post*, April 16, 2010. www.huffingtonpost.com.

60. Axelrad, "Losing My Book Advance Taught Me to Write."

61. Tracy McVeigh, "Britain's New Addicts: Women Who Gamble Online, at Home and in Secret," *Guardian* (Manchester), January 17, 2010. www.guardian.co.uk.

62. Quoted in McVeigh, "Britain's New Addicts."

Can People Recover from Online Addiction?

63. Quoted in Yao Minji, "Pulling the Plug," *Shanghai Daily*, September 23, 2009. www.china.org.cn.

64. Young, "How Do You Treat Internet Addiction?"

65. Quoted in Hunter R. Slaton, "Caught in the Web: An Internet Addict's Story," The Fix, March 27, 2012. www.thefix.com.

66. Roberts, "Confessions of a Cyber Junkie," p. 60.

67. Roberts, "Confessions of a Cyber Junkie," p. 60.

68. Nick, "What I Found Was an Understanding of Who I Am and What I Was Struggling With," ReSTART Young Adult Testimonials. www.netaddictionrecovery.com/young-adult-testimonial.html.

69. Nick, "What I Found Was an Understanding of Who I Am and What I Was Struggling With."

70. Christopher S. Stewart, "Obsessed with the Internet: A Tale from China," *Wired*, January 13, 2010. www.wired.com.

71. Quoted in Stewart, "Obsessed with the Internet."

List of Illustrations

Index

Note: Boldface page numbers indicate illustrations.

About the Author

Peggy J. Parks holds a bachelor of science degree from Aquinas College in Grand Rapids, Michigan, where she graduated magna cum laude. An author who has written over 100 educational books for children and young adults, Parks lives in Muskegon, Michigan, a town that she says inspires her writing because of its location on the shores of Lake Michigan.